How the Church Can

Minister to the World

Without Losing Itself

How the Church Can

BY LANGDON GILKEY

HARPER & ROW, PUBLISHERS

Minister to the World

Without Losing Itself

New York, Evanston, and London

To my parents

in loving appreciation

Geraldine Brown Gilkey

Charles Whitney Gilkey

Contents

Preface

This book on the contemporary church in America—its historical forms, its problems, and its possibilities—has grown slowly out of an interest generated at the Vanderbilt Divinity School. With a student body deeply loyal to the church and yet totally immersed in the problems of its relation to the surrounding culture, no theological teacher could long refrain from becoming concerned with this subject. For most of the facts and much of whatever wisdom may appear in this book I am indebted, therefore, first of all to successive classes of interested students, who in a course on the church studied, assessed, and pondered the forms of religion— and irreligion—which they found in their local parishes; and secondly, to the almost continual "bull session" on this subject carried on at lunch by that school's unusual faculty. The views here expressed took form gradually during the teaching of that course and then in lectures on this subject to various ministers' groups. Some of these thoughts were heard at a summer ministers' conference at Mission House Seminary in Plymouth, Wisconsin, in 1957; then, later, in the winter of 1962 in the McFadin lectures at Brite College of the Bible of Texas Christian University, and in the C. W. Chilton Lectures for the Missouri Christian Ministers' Conference held at the First Christian Church of Columbia, Missouri; and finally, in June of 1963, in the stimulating and, to both the lecturer and his wife, delightful School of Christian Studies at Meredith College in Raleigh, North Carolina. The entire series of chapters, in substantially its present form except for the last, was first presented as the Spring Lectures of 1963 at the College of the Bible in Lexington, Kentucky, where the kind reception given them encouraged their translation into book form. To my students and colleagues at Vanderbilt I am, therefore, especially grateful, and I wish further to thank all those hospitable and gracious people who were my hosts during the lectureships mentioned above. But to the helpful questions and continuous warm encouragement of my wife, Sonja, I owe most of all.

LANGDON GILKEY

The Divinity School
University of Chicago
October 23, 1963

1

The General Nature of the Problem

The subject of this book is the relation of the church to the world: how the church can minister to the world, which is its task, without losing itself, which is always its danger. Here we shall be concerned with the problem not so much on a theological or philosophical level, in the relation of science and philosophy to the doctrine and theology of the church, as on a practical level, that is, with the cultural world that surrounds our local churches and its bearing on their beliefs, behavior, experience, and worship. How is the *actual life* of our churches related to the culture in which we live?

Some sort of tension or opposition between the church and the world has always been part of the Christian faith. If this were not so, one might wonder what the church could have to say to the world that would be relevant to it. This fundamental tension —of opposition and at the same time of intense relevance—is reflected in almost all the major concepts of the New Testament: in the idea of the coming of the Son of God *into* the world to save it; in that of dying to sin and rising a *new* creature; in the radical ethic of the Sermon on the Mount, with its quite unworldly standards of human behavior; and, of course, in the strong eschatological consciousness of the early church.

Correspondingly, all through the centuries the church has in one way or another been conscious that, like its Lord, his teachings, and its own hopes, it is *in* but not *of* the world. As Augustine so eloquently said in the early fifth century, the roots and destiny of the church lie beyond the world in God's eternal will;[1] and its standards, while variously applicable and relevant to the world, are not merely the standards of the world. The church, then, if it is to be itself and do its work, must mediate to the world some Word, some Presence, some norm and standard, that are both transcendent in their origin—in some measure "holy"—and also relevant to the world's life. In a real sense the history of the church is the history, with all the errors and difficulties that sin and finitude create, of the search for this transcendence that is yet relevant, a search to embody and communicate the holy that will transform our lives.

When, with this fundamental character of the church before us, we look at the present state of American Protestant church life, certain unsettling questions come to mind. Is there in American Protestantism a living and real transcendence? Is there any sense of a transcendent Word that enlightens and forms the

[1] While in Augustine's thought the church as a "mixed" body of people is never identified with the Eternal City or community of God, nevertheless it is in his view of the apostolic church as the mystical Body of Christ that the church's eternal origin in God's will, its divine essence, and its heavenly destiny as the communion of saints are first and most clearly expressed. For, as he continually reiterates, the church is the Body of Christ the Son of God, and thus filled with His grace and destined to ascend with Him: "The whole Christ is Head and Body . . . the Head is our Savior Himself . . . But His body is the Church, not this one or that, but spread throughout the whole world . . . For the whole Church, which consists of all the faithful, since all the faithful are members of Christ, hath that Head set in Heaven, and it governeth His body. And although it is separated from our vision, yet it is joined together in charity. Hence the whole Christ is Head and its Body." In Ps. LVI, 1, found in E. Przywara, *An Augustinian Synthesis* (London: Sheed and Ward, 1945), p. 218. And the love or caritas which unites Christians to their Lord and so to his Body the church, is itself given to men only through the eternal election of God: "As, therefore, that one man was predestinated to be our Head, so we being many are predestinated to be His members." *On the Predestination of the Saints*, Chap. XXXI, found in W. J. Oates, ed., *The Basic Writings of St. Augustine* (New York: Random House, 1948), Vol. II, pp. 805-806. And so in the eternal will of God the church is formed: "This race we

church and its life, any real sense of the presence of God in worship, of a transcendent standard by which the church measures
its own ethical life and the behavior of its people? Is there any
real element of the holy in our contemporary churches?

All around us we see the church well acclimated to culture:
successful, respected, wealthy, full, and growing. But are the
transcendent and the holy there? In the area of belief we find
widespread indifference to the Bible and ignorance of its contents—and strong resentment if a biblical word of judgment is
brought to bear on the life of the congregation. In worship we
find notably lacking any sense of the holy presence of God and
of what worship is for—what it means and what value it may
have for God or man. In ethics we find the cultural ideals of
friendliness and fellowship more evident than the difficult standards of the New Testament or historic Christendom. Sadly
enough, the evidence supports the cynic who said that the church
in American society is the easiest club to enter and the hardest
from which to be expelled. This rootedness of the church in the
culture of our South, for instance, is vividly apparent to any
Northern visitor—but the same embeddedness in local worldly
culture equally characterizes American Protestantism wherever it
is. A seminary student at Vanderbilt once asked how he could
most easily remove an elder who used alcohol as manifestly too
"worldly" for an official position in the church. He became conscious for the first time of the depth of the problem of the
church in culture when he was asked whether this church, which
desired no "worldly" elders, was also segregated—as the world
is.

Such examples indicate a point we all recognize, namely, that
our American churches, conservative and liberal alike, are in
danger of merely reproducing in pious form the cultural world
(especially that of suburbia) that surrounds them. And the reason
is that they have, in the process of growth, lost that relation to
the transcendent which alone can make them relevant and crea-

have distributed into two parts, the one consisting of those who live according to man, the other of those who live according to God. And these
we also mystically call the two cities, or the two communities of men, of
which the one is predestined to reign eternally with God, and the other
to suffer eternal punishment with the devil." The City of God, Bk. XV,
Chap. i, ibid., Vol. I, p. 275.

tive in our national life. These chapters are an attempt to analyze
and understand how it is that our Protestant denominations have
become so vulnerable to the cultural influences among which
they are set, and then, on the basis of the most significant biblical
symbols of the church, briefly to suggest ways of dealing with
this situation.

We can, I think, most easily begin to understand the problem
of the contemporary church if we adopt the categories of
Troeltsch and use them to interpret our situation. Then we can
say that the predominant form of the American church is the
denomination, and that this is best understood as the *sect* type
within culture—a new amalgamation of the historic church-type
and sect-type churches, raising therefore quite new problems.

In his great historial study Ernst Troeltsch points out that,
roughly through the eighteenth century, there were two very
different interpretations of the tension between the church and
the world which expressed themselves in widely differing forms
of the church.[2] The first he called the *church-type* of the church,
illustrated by Roman Catholicism, by classic Lutheranism, and by
the Church of England. Here the church possesses a vast, unified,
and universal organizational structure which is intimately related
to the political power of its society and so becomes "established"
as the supreme spiritual force in the community. It thus governs
the spiritual life of all people in society, with the intent of bringing them all, high or low, rich or poor, respected or outcast,
virtuous or criminal, within reach of its truth, grace, and salvation. Correspondingly, its members are participating citizens of
the secular social realm: in medieval society they were the kings,
earls, dukes, knights, traders, soldiers, peasants, and hangmen.
The membership of the church was the medieval world in all its
worldliness; the layman in the church was thus a man in and of
the world in his ideas and attitudes. Inevitably this form of the
church must compromise with the world in many ways, especially in the moral standards it holds up to its laity. Here to be a
lay member does not necessarily mean to be personally holy,

[2] Ernst Troeltsch, *The Social Teachings of the Christian Churches* (New
York: The Macmillan Co., 1949), Vols. I and II, but especially Vol. I, pp.
328-82. This work is also available in a Harper Torchbook, 1960.

loving, selfless, pacifistic, humble, and so on; the layman, being in the world, is expected to accumulate moderate wealth, fight wars, support law and order, marry, and raise children.[3] There was little that was holy, in either theory or practice, in the behavior patterns of the medieval laity. The ordinary member of the "church-type" church relates himself to the holy in Christian life, not by saintliness, but by participating in the activity of the great church—a church whose holiness lies not in each man's personal behavior but elsewhere: in its apostolic authority, its sacraments, its dogmas, and its monastic establishment.

The obvious ethical compromises of "established" churches with the standards and behavior patterns of the world are often taken by free churchmen as certain proof that these churches have capitulated to the world, losing that necessary element of transcendence without which religion cannot live. This judgment is in error. For the church-type maintains its holiness and a strong opposition to the world in other areas of its life. Certain essential elements of the church are rigidly separated from the world and from all control or even influence by the cultural environment. In these central areas the layman, symbolizing the "world," has no authority at all; nor can the world's ideas or standards affect this separated core of the church's existence. In Catholicism these separated, holy elements are the controlling apostolic clergy, the sacraments, canon law, the dogmas, and the monastic orders;[4] in Lutheranism they are reduced to the Word as pure

[3] In Roman Catholic ethical theory the layman is required to live according to the "natural law" of justice, moderation (temperance), courage, and prudence, and not by the "counsels of perfection," those higher standards of purely Christian living which are derived from the New Testament and are made possible by the "gifts of the spirit," and which are applicable only to the life of the celibate clergy and the monastic orders. Of course the layman needs also the "theological virtues" of faith, hope, and charity in order to gain his supernatural destiny; but his life in the world is guided by the natural law, an expression of the inherent order of man's natural, rational, and communal capacities, whose particular embodiment is provided by his social context. See Thomas Aquinas, *Summa Theologica*, questions 61-70, especially question 69, art. 3.

[4] The sole ground in Catholic theory for the "holiness" of these various objective elements of the visible church (priesthood, sacraments, law, dogmas, etc.) is, of course, the basic belief that the church is the Mystical Body of Christ in which He dwells as the Head, and that His presence empowers, sanctifies, and so directs all the regularized and official acts of the church carried on by its clergy—viz., teaching (dogma), worship (sacra-

doctrine and the Eucharist; in Calvinism, to doctrine and the divinely given law. In each case these separated holy elements are "objective," "divinely given," "absolute," and so quite changeless.[5] They are never compromised, manipulated, tested, or reconceived; rather they are carefully treasured and conserved as providing whatever grace, truth, and authority reside in the church. These separated elements are the locus of the "holy"; they bear throughout the changing turmoil of secular culture the church's transcendence of the world, and so its tension with it. Although they are, through the church, *in* the world, these aspects of the church's life are, at least in theory, utterly uninfluenced by it. With remarkably few changes, the dogmas, the clerical and monastic life, the sacraments, and the canon law of the Roman

---

ments), and ruling (law). Hence these acts and their consequences are "holy," i.e., supernatural in origin, saving in effect, and quite infallible in character. Cf. George D. Smith, *The Teaching of the Catholic Church* (London: Burns, Oates and Washbourne, 1952), Chaps. XIX, XX, esp. pp. 710-24. Cf. also Karl Adam, *The Spirit of Catholicism* (New York: The Macmillan Co., 1952), Chaps. II, III, and XI.

[5] The Lutheran sense of the holiness of the Word, and so of the infallibility and changelessness of "right doctrine," has its roots in Luther himself, as the following illustrates: "One [a pastor] does not conduct his life and work as a private affair; but since he deals with God's Word, he speaks as a minister of the Word. A preacher knows this. He is sure that the doctrine is correct and that he has a divine office, that in the congregation he enters the office of God . . . Thus St. Paul is confident (2 Cor. 13:3) that he is speaking not his own word, but the Word of the Lord Christ. Thus we, too, can say that He has put it into our mouth. We have not invented it ourselves, but He has given it to us. If we have Christ's Word and speak it, then we also have this confidence . . . Here, where His Word is, everything is clear and good, but concerning our life we dare not boast. Concerning our speech we should boast before God and men of our certainty that our teaching is correct . . . This is evident from the fact that it builds upon the Lord Christ, it lets God be our Lord God, and it gives God the glory. This teaching is correct, and it cannot go wrong; nor will anyone improve on it." "Psalm 26," commentary, found in J. Pelikan, ed., *Luther's Works* (St. Louis, Mo.: Concordia, 1955), Vol. 12, pp. 186-87. That Calvin agrees with this view of doctrine as divinely given and thus irrefutable and changeless is evident in many places, e.g., "But before I reply [to an objection against his doctrine of Providence] I wish the reader again to be apprized that this cavil is directed, not against me, but against the Holy Spirit, who dictated to the pious Job this confession, that what had befallen him had happened according to the Divine will . . ." John Calvin, *Institutes of the Christian Religion*, trans. by J. Allen, Bk. I, Chap. XVIII, sec. 3 (Philadelphia: Presbyterian Board of Christian Education, 1936), Vol. I, p. 257.

Catholic Church have lasted in the world for centuries, providing in that remarkable institution its undeniable sense of holiness and of the real presence of the supernatural. Because of these elements removed from all compromise, the church-type can afford the dangerous compromises with worldliness which it allows in the area of lay behavior, and in the political and social privileges granted to its established clergy. It is these latter that free church-men see when they call established churches "worldly"; it is the former, the separated elements, that Catholics see when they call the church "holy."

The second great form of the church is commonly called the *sect-type* of church. There have been many illustrations of this form in church history, from the Montanists of the second century to Jehovah's Witnesses and the Amish of our contemporary scene. It was, however, from the sixteenth through the latter part of the eighteenth century that this form of the church was most significant and widespread. Its clearest examples were the Anabaptists or Spiritualists (later the Mennonites) of Reformation Europe, the Quakers of seventeenth- and eighteenth-century England and America, and the Continental and English Baptists of the same period, the Independents, and other assorted radical groups of the English Civil War,[6] as well as the Campbellites (who later split into the Disciples of Christ and the Churches of Christ[7]) of early nineteenth-century America. But sectarian em-

[6] Troeltsch, *op. cit.*, Vol. II, pp. 691-787.

[7] That the early Disciples of Christ belong within the general category of "sect-type" churches is, I think, unquestionable. The rationalistic milieu of the Enlightenment, of course, made it impossible for them to appeal to the inner workings of the Holy Spirit as the "holy" in religion as had earlier Spiritualists, Baptists, and Quakers; and their acceptance of the social order divested their ethic of most of its socially critical elements. Nevertheless, their fundamental principles, as enunciated in the "Last Will and Testament" inspired by Barton Stone, and the "Declaration and Address" inspired by Thomas and Alexander Campbell, are clearly sectarian. Thus: (1) The church is not a hierarchical institution, but a congregation of adult Christians who have made individual professions of faith, have been baptized, and are obedient to that faith. (2) The sole authority for the life and practice of the church is the Bible, interpreted as outlining a law for the Christian community. (3) There are no ecclesiastical differences between Christians, and so no need for the distinction of lay and clerical. Each man should believe for himself and on the basis of his own reading of the Bible. (4) There are no sacred dogmas or creeds binding on the church or the Christian—rather, churchly traditions have divided men in-

phases and principles may be found in many Protestant groups not so clearly sectarian in origin—for example, among the American Methodists and the Congregationalists.[8] As we shall see, many of the principles that now go to make up the denominational form of the church, so common in America today, have their ultimate origin in sectarian church life.

Consistently throughout its history, this form of the church has represented a totally different solution to the problem of its relation to the world from that of the established churches. In their clearest form, in the sixteenth- and seventeenth-century Anabaptist, Baptist, and Quaker groups, the church was understood as a gathered community of adult, convinced, and personally committed Christians—"gathered" from out of the world by a personal inward experience of grace, and separated from the world's ways by their rigorous following of a very unworldly interpretation of the gospel ethic.[9]

---

stead of uniting them. (5) The requirements for a Christian are solely that he profess faith in Christ and obey him according to the Scriptures; and members are retained in the community only so long as their conduct is in accord with this profession. Here, then, is a community of adult lay Christians, gathered by their faith in the Bible and their ethical obedience to it, and recognizing over their religious lives the authority of no hierarchy, doctrine, or state. This is a rationalistic, "Enlightenment" form of the general sectarian movement.

[8] The debate as to what form of church the Methodists represent is, of course, interminable and the issues complex; manifestly numerous "church-type" characteristics are evident in the Anglican John Wesley and in many of his like-minded followers, especially in England. All I seek to maintain in these remarks is that certain sectarian principles (e.g., the emphasis on personal experience in religion, and especially on ethical perfection) are also evident in Wesley and in Methodism, especially in America, though I should not go as far as Troeltsch in placing them within the general sectarian category (op. cit., Vol. II, pp. 721-26).

[9] The classic expression of this view of the church as a gathered community of adults who have personally experienced grace and who accordingly live separated from the world, is the Schleitham Confession of Faith, written by Swiss Anabaptists in 1527. The first article, on baptism, expresses the sectarian insistence on personal religion for membership in the church; and the fourth, on separation, the need for its ethical results. First: "Baptism shall be given to all those who have learned repentance and amendment of life, and who believe truly that their sins are taken away by Christ, . . . This excludes all infant baptism. . . . Fourth. We are agreed (as follows) on separation: A separation shall be made from the evil and from the wickedness which the devil planted in the world; in this manner, simply that we shall not have fellowship with them and not run with them

The sect-type, therefore, emphasized individual, personal experience in religion: no man is a Christian unless he has himself experienced redemption through the work of the Holy Spirit, and unless he now exhibits this work in a transformed life.[10] This new life in the Spirit, above all, is what makes a man a Christian—not any priest's pronouncement over a baby or the layman's nominal obedience to doctrine. Thus the work of the Holy Spirit, rather than a creed or the sacramental authority of clergy, creates the church, empowers it, and brings in new members through adult conversion. In such a group all members are laymen, for no man can by outward office be closer to this inward work of the Spirit than any other. Consequently here there are no "clergy," with special holiness, special power, or special authority; there is at the most only the office of preacher and teacher, a kind of *primus inter pares* among the faithful.[11] Nor are any sacred theological dogmas needed or tolerated. Through the work of the

---

in the multitude of their abominations. . . . For truly all creatures are in but two classes, good and bad, believing and unbelieving, darkness and light, the world and those who have come out of the world . . . and none can have part with the other." The confession goes on to require of members rejection of all established churches, "drinking houses and civic affairs" (an interesting fusing of the vices with the structures of society), "the un-Christian, devilish weapons of force," the use of the civil courts, the vocation of magistrates, and all use of oaths. This confession may be found in H. E. Fosdick, *Great Voices of the Reformation* (New York: Random House, 1952), pp. 286-95.

Or again, from Menno Simons (1496-1561): "Christ's Church consists of the chosen of God, His saints and beloved who have washed their robes in the blood of the Lamb, who are born of God and led by Christ's Spirit, who are in Christ and Christ in them, who hear and believe His Word, live in their weakness according to His commandments and in patience and meekness follow in His footsteps, who hate evil and love the good, earnestly desiring to apprehend Christ as they are apprehended of Him. For all who are in Christ are new creatures, flesh of His flesh, bone of His bone and members of His body . . ." *Ibid.*, p. 316.

[10] "To be a Christian is to be in measure like Christ, and to be ready to be offered as He gave Himself to be offered. I do not say we are perfect as Christ was perfect, but I say rather we seek the perfection which Christ never lost . . . All Christians in whom the Holy Spirit lives, that is, all real Christians, are one with Christ in God and are like Christ." Hans Denck, quoted *ibid.*, p. 312.

[11] See the description of "true ministers" in Dietrick Phillips, "The Church of God" (1560) found in G. H. Williams, *Spiritual and Anabaptist Writers*, Library of Christian Classics, Vol. 25 (Philadelphia: Westminster Press, 1957), pp. 240-42.

Spirit each man understands the gospel as he reads it for himself in the Bible; he needs no official ecclesiastical interpretation to guide his mind. Nor, in such an inward, personal form of religion, is there room for an objectively holy sacrament as the central channel of relation to God. Such outward, physical mediation of the divine through sacrament or rite is, like the official authority of the priest or the codified statements of a dogma, abhorrent to the sectarian consciousness. For all relations to the divine are inward, not external; personal, not objective; since what is not experienced inwardly cannot be holy.[12] All else leads, at best, to a formal sterility of religion, and at the worst, to authoritarian tyranny. Thus the sectarian form rejected the authority of clergy and of religious doctrine and denied that an external sacrament could of itself be a medium for the holy. All those aspects of the church-type which, as we have seen, separated it from the world —ecclesiastical hierarchy, sacred dogma, holy sacraments, and monastic ethics—were vigorously negated, and are still, by these other groups.

In its own way, however, the sect no less than the church-type made no compromise with culture. It maintained its "holiness," its opposition to the world, in two other significant ways: by the rigid requirements of its own special ethical and communal life,[13] and by its absolute fidelity in the realm of the mind to the

[12] The best expression of this inward definition of the "holy" as against all outward media whatsoever is found, of course, among the Quakers, to whom, originally at least, not only were dogmas, sacraments, and clergy anathema, but even simple liturgical devices and church buildings. Cf. this example from George Fox: "For the steeple houses [church buildings] and pulpits were offensive to my mind, because both priests and people called them the house of God, and idolized them, reckoning that God dwelt there in the outward house. Whereas they should have looked for God and Christ to dwell in their hearts, and their bodies to be made the temples of God; for the apostle said, 'God dwelleth not in temples made with hands': but by reason of the people's idolizing these places, it was counted an heinous thing to declare against them." *Journal,* J. L. Nickalls, ed., (Cambridge, Eng.: Cambridge University Press, 1952), p. 85.

[13] The strictness of the moral and religious rules in sectarian communities is measured by the vehemence and seriousness with which their leaders defended the use of "the ban," that is the power in the community to expel a member for moral or religious misbehavior. For example, cf. Menno Simons, "On the Ban," and Ulrich Stadler, "Cherished Instructions on Sin, Excommunication, and the Community of Goods," Moravia, 1537, in Williams, *op. cit.,* pp. 263-84. This power of removal from the community for moral failures has been a typically sectarian motif since the earliest days of

Bible. Here, in the area of its communal patterns of behavior and its communal intellectual life, the world could not enter. As gathered communities of dedicated Christians, brought "out of the worldly world," the sects rejected practically *in toto* the world's ethics as well as its philosophy and science, and they looked with more than suspicion on the creations of literature and art within the culture. Though in most cases they lived physically in society, in almost every significant spiritual sense the majority of these groups rejected not only the vices of culture but culture itself. Thus in behavior they refused to accumulate personal property, to take oaths, to use or in some cases even to obey the courts, to fight in war, to employ force in any way to defend themselves (even, in the sixteenth century, to carry a sword for their own defense), or to accept political office or social privilege.[14] And in almost all cases their sole intellectual

the church, indicating, as writers in every generation have emphasized, that for these groups the holiness of the church as a community depends upon the preservation of the purity of its members, so that no "impure" members may be tolerated. Wherever such powers of excommunication for moral faults appear, therefore, a sectarian principal has been uncovered: namely, that the community itself is holy through the moral behavior of its members. At this point, if nowhere else, both Calvinism (cf. the *Institutes,* Bk. IV, Chap. 12, and *The Catechism of the Church in Geneva*) and Methodism can be said to approach a sectarian viewpoint.

This position is, of course, in sharp contrast to the Catholic (Augustinian) and Lutheran doctrines that the church as a body of people is not at all holy but a mixture of the godly and the ungodly, of "sheep and goats," "wheat and tares," whose holiness lies (as we saw) in its holy sacraments and/or holy doctrines. Calvin's position on this matter is very complex: on the one hand, he held that the church is filled with both the elect and the reprobate (*Institutes*, Bk. IV, Chap. I, secs. 2, 3, *ibid.*, Vol. II, pp. 270-73); but on the other hand, he believed in real sanctification, in church discipline, and so in excommunication of all patently immoral members, to the end that the community in which the Lord's Supper is observed may be holy and show forth the glory of God.

[14] Cf. the following eloquent description of the Anabaptist mode of life: "Our manner of life, our customs and conversation, are known everywhere to all. Rather than wrong any man of a single penny, we would suffer the loss of a hundred gulden; and sooner than strike an enemy with the hand, much less with the spear, or sword, or halbert, as the world does, we would die and surrender life. We carry no weapon, neither spear nor gun, as is clear as the open day; and they who say that we have gone forth by thousands to fight, they lie and impiously traduce us to our rulers." From "A Protest from the Anabaptists of Moravia against Deportation," Fosdick, *op. cit.,* p. 305.

And with regard to its "unworldly" economic behavior, the sectarian

fare was the Bible rather than dramas, essays, novels, or other belles-lettres.

The basic character of a form of the church can usually be found if one asks: How does this form of the church understand the holy, and through what media does it regard it as coming to men? This is manifestly true of the sects as a type of the church. Holiness to the sect could not be the attribute of anything objective, such as a doctrine, a clerical office, or a physical element of a sacrament. It must be the quality alone of a personal life in its inward beliefs, feelings, and experience, and in its outward behavior. Obviously such a view affected the modes of worship, which were radically purified of all objective holy liturgical forms and symbols, and very nearly stripped of the concrete media of Word and sacraments.

Even more was this interpretation of holiness felt in the ethical patterns of the life of the sect. If a community was to be holy, every member of it in his total behavior and thinking must reflect

---

ideal was as follows: "But it, that is, such a community must move about in this world, poor, miserable, small and rejected of the world, of whom, however, the world is not worthy. Whoever strives for the lofty things [of this world] does not belong. Thus in this community everything must proceed equally, all things be one and communal, alike in the bodily gifts of their Father in heaven . . . In brief, 'one,' 'common' builds the Lord's house and is pure; but 'mine,' 'thine,' 'his,' 'own' divides the Lord's house and is impure. Therefore, where there is ownership and one has it, and it is his, and one does not wish to be one with Christ and his own in living and dying, he is outside of Christ and his communion and thus has no Father in heaven." Ulrich Stadler, *op. cit.,* pp. 277-78.

The same emphasis on self-sacrificial obedience as the mark of the Christian, and on consequent separation from the world's ways, reappears in the Quakers: "Friend, Thou dost profess God and Christ in words, see how thou dost follow Him. To take off burdens, to visit them that are in prison, and show mercy, clothe thy own flesh, and deal thy bread to the hungry; these are God's commandments. To relieve the fatherless, and to visit the widows in their afflictions, and to keep thyself uppspotted of the world; this is pure religion before God . . ." Fox, *op. cit.,* p. 54. "And major Porter proffered the oath of allegiance to me to take and I told him I never took oath in my life of one side or the other, against or for myself, but did abide in Christ's doctrine, who said, 'Swear not at all,' and did suffer in that." *Ibid.,* p. 381. "That the spirit of Christ, by which we are guided, is not changeable, so as once to command us from a thing as evil and again to move unto it; and we do certainly know, and so testify to the world, that the spirit of Christ, which leads us into all truth, will never move us to fight and war against any men with outward weapons, neither for the Kingdom of Christ, nor for the kingdoms of this world." *Ibid.,* pp. 399-400.

the divine will. This is the root of the sect community's separateness from the world in its modes of life and thought, and of its rejection of worldly habits of violence and coercion, wealth and rank, as well as of vice. Since holiness is the attribute of a total life, every aspect of that life must be holy, none can be worldly. The absolute standards of the gospel ethic are thus applied by the sect to each Christian member, clerical or lay (and this distinction almost disappears), and what is more, to every aspect of his life—social relations as well as personal habits. For such a view, participation in a social structure that involves patterns of coercion or violence or cruelty—such as slavery, war, or segregation[15]—and is thus against the gospel ethic of love, is as morally compromising as carousing. The ethic of love and purity is here applied to all of life, but without hope of transforming the social structure within which the world moves. Like the monastics, in their own way these groups retired to form separate social organ-

[15] The clearest early expression that a social structure, judged by the law of the gospel, is wrong and therefore cannot longer be borne, comes from the "Twelve Articles" of the Schwabian peasants with regard to slavery (1525): "Third, it has been the custom hitherto for men to hold us as their own property; and this is pitiable, seeing that Christ has redeemed and bought us all with the precious sheding of his blood, the lowly as well as the great, excepting no one. Therefore, it agrees with scripture that we be free and will to be so. Not that we would be entirely free; God does not teach us that we should desire no rulers." These articles may be found in *Works of Martin Luther*, Vol. IV (Philadelphia: Muhlenberg Press, 1931), pp. 210-16. As H. Richard Niebuhr points out, it is no accident that this early Christian criticism of slavery appeared amongst those who themselves were oppressed by that institution—just as, in a later generation, the Christian antipathy to segregation is most clearly felt by the Negroes who suffer from it, while its evils are overlooked by the whites who profit by them. See H. Richard Niebuhr, *Social Sources of Denominationalism* (Hamden, Conn.: Shoe String Press, 1954), Chap. III.

As far as the author knows, the best contemporary example of the social protest aspect of sectarian religion has been the Koinonia community in Americus, Georgia. Convinced that the segregated pattern of life in America, and especially in the South, are utterly antithetical to the gospel, which requires a total rather than an occasional and token obedience to its command of brotherhood, this group withdrew from ordinary social existence, formed its own community of farming and living, and there patterned its life on the interracial standards it regarded as obligatory to genuine Christianity. An observer of the commitment, as well as the sufferings, of this group finds himself awed by their fidelity and integrity, and himself ashamed in comparison by his own halfhearted and fitful obedience. The sad ironies of this situation and its terminal history are many, but two may be mentioned. First, in most cases the culturally "established"

isms within which the holy life could be lived, accepting from the world only its habits of householding, trading, marrying, and begetting children, but like the monks eschewing personal wealth, power, and all violence.

The significant result of this view of holiness and its consequent theme of separation was that the layman in sectarian groups was not, as in the established churches, *in* the world, participating in the world's structures of power and dominated alike by its behavior patterns and its opinions. In his relation to the world he was more like a priest or monk of the church-type than like a modern layman. For he was a consecrated, committed individual, separated from worldly life in the content of his thought and in his standards of behavior, learned in his faith (for he read the Bible constantly), taking seriously the requirements of a personal religious life in private devotions and family prayers, and directed in every significant detail of daily activity by what he regarded as absolute Christian law. The similarity between monk or priest and the sectarian layman, and the difference between the sectarian layman and the modern denominational layman, is almost the crux of the church's present difficulty, and certainly of my remarks. It is clear that the repudiation by sect-type churches of sacred dogmas and sacraments, ecclesiastical authority and monastic perfection, did *not* mean in their case (as Catholics often assume) the triumph of a secular culture over these forms of the church—any more than the compromising ethic of Catholicism, as the free churchman thinks, spells the same. Rather, in the sects the community itself, in both its life and its thought, was separated and holy. It was dominated, not

and so ethically compromising—i.e., totally segregated—churches from which this group "separated" in order to bear its Christian witness (and from whose members they suffered persecution) are the Baptist, Methodist, and Disciples churches of Georgia, descendants of the sectarian movements of another day and clime but rulers of the present age. And secondly, in the "freedom-loving" world of our modern denominational culture there was so little room for real sectarian protest against that culture that the community (if it was to survive) finally had to move its locus to New Jersey, where it really ceases to be a sect. In contrast to the sixteenth and seventeenth centuries in which, as every schoolboy knows, established religions were "tyrannical" but many sects survived and kept their identity, in our day few forms of religion can resist the omniverous maw of our monolithic culture.

by the world's ways and ideas, but by an absolute ethic and a revealed world-view derived almost entirely from biblical sources. Again essential elements of the church have been separated, removed, and so kept holy: in this case, both the communal and the intellectual life of the sectarian group itself.

The question we must now ask ourselves is: How does the denomination, as we find it around us in America, resolve this problem of its relation to the world? What elements, if any, are holy—transcendent—separated? Are there any? Are there none? Has there been so complete an amalgamation of church and world that this relation is no longer even felt to be a problem?

First of all, it is clear that in the contemporary denomination we find a new type of relationship between the church and its culture, and this raises real problems, as it also opens out immense possibilities. The denomination represents a new form of the church because it has borrowed and then combined essential traits of both the preceding forms. Like the church-type, the denomination is intimately related to the world. Members of modern churches are men and women very much *in* the world. The leading laity, like the dukes, earls, soldiers, and peasants of the Middle Ages, are the governors and workers of modern society: bankers, managers, industrialists, brokers, engineers, lawyers, and doctors—if we can only get them to come in! They participate in politics as voters, if not as officials; and somewhat ironically, an older sectarian form such as the Disciples is proud when one of its members becomes Vice-President! They use the courts of secular government (as do our churches themselves), and own property, direct business and economic affairs, and protect and increase their personal wealth. They play the world's sports and enjoy its amusements. Some denominational church people may once upon a time have balked at the stage and at movies, and some still hesitate to enjoy the world's smaller vices. But TV in the home has broken down many of the older entertainment bans,[16] and fewer and fewer laymen are concerned in a

[16] Of all the prohibitions of the long sectarian tradition, none is more ancient and honorable than that against attendance at the theater and later the movies; and even more against the vocation of acting. For this old tradition, the stage has represented the essence of worldliness, the actors' troupe being only slightly more admissible than the society of the race track. Nothing indicates more clearly, therefore, the acceptance of "the

Christian way (though they may be medically roused) about the "minor" vices of smoking, card-playing, and drinking. It would never occur to the modern layman, be he staunch Baptist, Campbellite, or Methodist, to refuse political office, the use of the courts for personal or business grievances, or an honest opportunity to make a profit; or not to send off his minister to be a chaplain in the armed forces—all of which would have horrified his sectarian forefathers. Finally, the children of denominational families, however conservative the family theology, are educated in the world's schools and thence imbibe something, at least, of modernity's science, snatches of its *Weltanschauung*, and almost all of its values. Thus in the basic areas having to do with the relation of lay life to the world, i.e., in areas where the sects used to be separated from the world—in their modes of communal behavior and moral customs, and in the biblical content of their thought—our denominations are "church-type" churches. Their members are *in* culture, and the characteristics of their moral life, their values and goals, and their world-view, are alike culturally determined.

---

world" and amalgamation with it than the gradual erosion of this prohibition and the appearance of erstwhile sectarians on TV and in the movies. The career of Pat Boone, loyal member of the Church of Christ, is instructive at this point. He began as a good sectarian would, wary of "sin" in the movie world and in his vocation of acting in particular, and above all wary of portraying a "sinful" character; thus he would not smoke, drink, or kiss in his roles. Apparently, however, this proved an impediment to his career, so widely extolled among his proud fellow church members in Nashville, who had by now accepted movies and TV shows as "good" things. So Pat began to play different kinds of roles, now portraying tough, hard-drinking, moll-shifting teen-age hoods. That he had to explain this new Pat to his Church of Christ friends in several local articles is evidence of his older sectarian heritage; but that he could now justify these "sinful" roles by the arguments that (a) some teen-ager might thereby be helped, and (b) he would play the role "sincerely," shows how far the integrity of the acting profession and of the entertainment world it serves have come to be accepted by these sectarian groups.

Two other examples illustrate this movement of sects into culture, as previously rejected elements of cultural life gradually come to seem "normal" and thus "innocent." A Nazarene student told the writer that his mother-in-law, who had never set foot in a movie theater, had welcomed TV into her home. "It can't be all that bad here in my Christian living room," she said. "And what's wrong with that nice Mr. Welk and Mr. Linkletter, and those interesting quiz programs?" (This was before 1958.) Soon, needless to say, she was contentedly keeping the set turned on

On the other hand, the American denomination is sectarian in heritage, and thus both the theoretical polity and many of the practical structures of its church life tend to be sectarian in character.[17] Any sense that clerical office of itself carries authority is almost nonexistent. On the contrary, lay participation in the life of the church has been emphasized in all our communions, and in more than a few denominations complete lay control over the local church and its minister has been effectively realized. There has also been a strong de-emphasis of the objective holiness of sacrament, liturgy, and doctrine, and the significance of these has practically disappeared from denominational life. Although its organization and staff have multiplied, the denomination has shown little interest in a sacred hierarchical ecclesiastical system or an authoritarian or sacerdotal clergy—there being no sacred sacraments, sacred law, or sacred dogmas for such a separated class of men to preserve and administer. Like the sects, denominational Christianity emphasizes the personal Christian faith and high moral life of each individual in the church. This personal commitment and virtue appear as the sole purpose of

---

to watch the late shows, and when her son-in-law rather meanly asked how she could bring herself to look at movies, she replied that in this case none of her good money was going to that wicked Hollywood.

Just before writing this note the writer returned from a trip through Indiana where, at a roadside cafe, he and his wife encountered two "Dunker" couples, the men with spade beards and homemade shirts, suits, and haircuts, and the women with white lace caps and black Mother Hubbards, all four busily enjoying hamburgers with cokes. The on-again, off-again relation to culture of such contemporary sectarian groups reached a new pitch of confusion, however, when the four left their all-American meal and climbed into their new 1963 white Buick Le Sabre sedan.

Another clerical Buick may be noted here. Driving at no snail's pace, recently, down the Connecticut turnpike, the writer was passed as if motionless by a coal-black 1963 Buick Riviera, driven by a black-robed Roman cleric in a white straw skimmer. The sheer elegance of this clerical ensemble was matched, apparently, only by its political and social status, for the Massachusetts license plate, also coal-black, was marked solely by an eloquent white "X." If General Motors' Buick Division represents the essence as well as the apex of what may be called "American culture," then the fact that leading members of these historically widely divergent groups now tour the freeways in elegant Buicks has no small religious and social significance.

[17] I have said "theoretical" polity and "many" of its practical structures because, as I shall try to show in Chap. 2, most of our denominations have in actual practice unconsciously taken on certain significant church-type

Christianity, and their presence or absence in the congregation provide the sole standard for any "holiness" a church may have. We should note, however, how different are the modern denominational demands as regards this personal holiness from what they were in an earlier sectarian form of the church. For now, except in fringe groups, a "Christian" moral life no longer implies a propertyless, pacifistic existence separated from the political, economic, and social structure of society. On the contrary, outside the church doors of the modern denomination, whether Baptist, Methodist, or even Church of Christ, line up the Cadillacs and Continentals of the mighty in our society. For this reason a denominational congregation in a contemporary urban or suburban center would seem unbelievably worldly to a typical sectarian; and surely the average modern, sophisticated Disciple or Methodist layman would look on the sectarian Amish or Jehovah's Witnesses as "queer" in their rejection of American culture. Yet in their common understanding of the church as a congregation of believing people, and so as lay-centered and nearly lay-controlled; in their common emphasis on personal religious experience and moral behavior as the sole loci of the holy; in their common rejection of liturgy, sacraments, and dogmas as media of the holy—and finally, in their mutual abhorrence of any authority beyond the individual and the free congregation in basic matters of faith and life, these two groups are clearly related and must be understood together.

American denominations which are sectarian in origin, such as the Baptists and the Campbellite churches, have merely carried over these principles of church life from their own past into their present denominational life. Other denominations, with other origins, have found themselves moved inexorably toward lower and lower forms of sacrament, liturgy, doctrinal authority, and clerical status, and toward more and more emphasis on the voluntary, personal, moral, and communal aspects of religious life. The result is that services in most (though not all) Congregational, Presbyterian, Baptist, Episcopal, and Methodist churches

---

characteristics (see also n. 18, below). It remains true, however, that the official theory of the denominations, the image they have of themselves, and very many of their objective structural forms are sectarian in character, as the present text seeks to show.

are much the same in form and content, and the problems of their church life are fundamentally similar. The denominational form and its relation to our culture has standardized our churches to such a degree that, unless we move quite out of the great middle class—or out of the country itself—most of our churches are, in these essentials of thought, behavior, and worship, indistinguishable from one another.[18]

Here, then, we have in the denomination the sect-type *in* Christendom, *in* culture.[19] The separated community has become the community church, related inherently and intentionally to the world. This new form creates the present possibility of the transformation of the world of which it is now fully a part. Unhappily, it is also the source of most of our serious problems. As we have noted, this new form preserves no essential area separate or removed from cultural domination. Unlike the church-type, it has no sacred hierarchy, no holy sacraments, no holy dogmas; and yet, unlike the sects, it possesses no separated communal, moral, and intellectual life. Having no separated areas which

[18] This is, of course, the conclusion of Will Herberg's remarkable book on American religion, *Protestant, Catholic, Jew* (Garden City, N.Y.: Doubleday Anchor, 1960), Chaps. 5 and 10. See also Obenhaus' "conclusion," after an exhaustive analysis of the churches and their life in a rural county in Iowa: "If the Corn County analysis has validity, there is decreasing difference in the ideologies and belief structure of the various denominations. In their place is a uniformity of religious belief and practice fostered by the same forces that make for uniformity in the rest of American society." Victor Obenhaus, *The Church and Faith in Mid-America* (Philadelphia: Westminster Press, 1963), p. 141.

In his excellent book on the sociological contours of the church as a human community, Gustafson points out how this drift toward uniformity among our denominations extends beyond the inner spirit to a surprising similarity of political structure, despite vast differences in official "polity" (i.e., theory of structure): "In spite of differences in formal polity, however, the denominational structures of American churches are moving towards a common pattern . . . The allotments of power and authority made in the past did not foresee the need for the growth of ecclesiastical organization at the state or regional level . . . Congregational and Presbyterian denominations find themselves with officers who function as bishops (i.e., the executive secretaries), not in the sense of elevated spiritual authorities, but in the sense of administrators of churches in a given area. Episcopal churches find their bishops functioning more and more as general administrators than as pastors and spiritual leaders in their dioceses." James Gustafson, *Treasure in Earthen Vessels* (New York: Harper & Row, 1961), pp. 38-39.

[19] Cf. Herberg's excellent statement of much the same thesis: "This

might be able to preserve the holy *from* the world, and thus be enabled to mediate the holy *to* the world, this church is in fact in imminent danger of being engulfed by the world.[20]

This volume, then, concerns the relation of the denominational church to its culture, and the vulnerability of its life to domination by the world. I am, in other words, raising in a somewhat new form the problem which the secularism of our era poses for the churches in our society.

The progressive secularization of our life in the last centuries needs no documentation. What cannot be overemphasized is the universality and depth of this phenomenon. In our century it has moved into every institutional structure, including the church, and it permeates every individual's thoughts and feelings—even, if we are honest, those of churchmen, clerics, and theologians. By secularization I mean the absence of the religious, transcendent, or ultimate dimension or reference in all the facets of life, and the consequent derivation of all standards and goals solely

---

means that outside the old world distinction of church and sect America has given birth to a new type of religious structure—the denomination . . . The denomination is the 'non-conformist sect' become central and normative. It differs from the church in the European understanding of the term in that it would never dream of claiming to be *the* national ecclesiastical institution; it differs from the sect in that it is socially established, thoroughly institutionalized, and nuclear to the society in which it is found." *Op. cit.*, pp. 85-86. See further Joachim Wach, "Church, Denomination, and Sect," in his *Types of Religious Experience* (London: Routledge and Kegan Paul, 1951), Chap. XI.

[20] The fear that the church reflects the surrounding culture more than its own transcendent source and norm is by no means new in studies of American religion. Herberg in the study cited makes this perhaps his main thesis, and both Lenski and Obenhaus came to this conclusion from their sociological studies of the contemporary church. "This, however, is very close to what Herberg had in mind when he stated his now familiar paradox that Americans are becoming more religious while at the same time becoming more secular. Despite attending the churches more frequently, their thoughts and values are less often derived from distinctly religious . . . sources and more often derived from secular sources. In short, a transcendental faith is gradually being transformed into a cultural faith . . . we might add that the pages of history are replete with the ruins of cultural religions which had the misfortune of subsequently encountering transcendental religions." Gerhard Lenski, *The Religious Factor* (Garden City, N.Y.: Doubleday Anchor, 1963), pp. 59-60.

from the natural and social environments in which men live. It is as if for our age the receiving set for religion had been tuned way down, or in some cases turned quite off. For multitudes of us (and they seem to be most characteristic of our time) no experience of God is either expected or felt, no word from God listened for or heard, and no command of God received or obeyed. To many the question of the existence or experience of these things is not even intelligible or meaningful. Most of us go about our lives quite as if there were no God at all, and until tragedy or something equally forceful strikes us, we do not notice this lack. In the ordinary course of life we Christians, lay, cleric, or theologian, make our daily decisions and judgments about people, events, and ourselves largely by standards borrowed from and shared with the society around us; we derive our joys from the natural environment and from the human relations among which we live here and now; and we surely plan our careers and our homes in the normally accepted terms of patriotic and professional existence in our communities. If we are theologically competent, we can of course formulate theological propositions and theories that make this otherwise secular existence coherent in terms of a wider, "religious" environment. But as we all readily admit, we have difficulty in pointing to concrete experiences that support these formulations, or to real changes in our lives or daily decisions that clearly flow from them. Even among preachers and theologians, therefore, the acids of secularism have penetrated to the very marrow, and a seminary community, like any local church, must now at its deepest level struggle with the sense of unreality and doubt that accompany this present elusiveness of the divine. As well as anyone among us, William Hamilton has described this situation:

We seem to be those who are trying to believe in a time of the death of God . . . and the cry of dereliction from the cross is sometimes the only biblical word that can speak to us . . . Perhaps we ought to conclude that the special Christian burden of our time is the situation of being without God. There is, for some reason, no possession of God for us, but only a hope, only a waiting. This is perhaps part of the truth: to be a Christian today is to stand, somehow, as a man without God but with hope. Faith is for many of us, we might say, purely eschatological. It is a kind of trust that one day he will no longer be absent from us. Faith is a cry to the absent God; faith is hope.[21]

Any discussion of the relation of the church to culture in our age must be set against the massive backdrop of this contemporary absence of God. The church now lives in a society for which God is elusive, if not quite unknown, and the categories of the holy and the transcendent are apparently meaningless, empty, and useless. And surely the deep religious problems of the church to which we will be alluding in these pages are caused in large part by the fact that this secular spirit has penetrated into the mind and heart of the church as well as permeating the world outside it.

Our first reaction as churchmen to this undoubted fact of modern life is, of course, to bemoan it. What could be worse than that the Lord's church be swamped by irreligion, radical doubt, and worldly values? But powerful lines of thought among Christians in recent years point us in quite another direction. For one thing, it is almost irrefutable that the long-range influence of secularism on the churches has been quite beneficial—almost, so to speak, "Christian." In fact, contemporary Christianity owes so much to its environment that a catalogue of secular influences reads almost like a list of the most creative elements of modern Christian thought and existence. Over the past four hundred years the church has learned from the secular world around it (not without resistance), among other things, a respect for science and the tentativeness of all truth; an active distaste for the concrete evils of this life and a concern to eradicate them; a tolerance of opposing communions and faiths; an acceptance of the joys and pleasures as well as the crises and sorrows of this life; a rejection of the legalism and creedalism

[21] William Hamilton, *The New Essence of Christianity* (New York: Association Press, 1961), pp. 58, 59, and 63-64. The most powerful recent expression, however, of this absence of God, of the total silence when we call upon Him, and the experiences of dereliction and emptiness that follow from that silence, has for this writer been the Ingmar Bergman film *Winter Light*. In this taut and stark study of a Swedish pastor, the latter is rendered infinitely weak and empty by comparison with the tougher, more honest folk around him, because his life continues to center around and consist of this now admittedly empty relation to a God who is not there. The sense of the outward, and consequent inward, emptiness of religion in our day is in this film quite overwhelming.

that were demonic elements in its own past—and one could name a good many more. Whether or not these gifts in turn have their root in the Hebrew-Christian faith is another—and in this situation a minor—matter, for the relevant point is that the church had to learn them from its secular antagonists. And there is every evidence that this learning process, and so the indebtedness of the church to the world, continues, whether in the depth of questions concerning human existence raised by modern secular literature, plays, and films, or the probing inquiries of secular philosophy as to the meanings, if any, of theological language. Thus our involuntary response of anguish is certainly uneducated and ungrateful, if not deliberately dishonest. Secularism has been a more incisive and certainly more faithful prophetic critic of the church than the church has been of the world. And if our churches preach a better gospel or live a more creative life now than in earlier dogmatic, moralistic, and intolerant days, then it is partly because of this criticism from the world around us.

Secondly, it seems by no means certain to some that a secularization of our theology might not free it for a more useful role in our common life. Is it not true, many churchmen are asking, that a supernatural gospel about a "God out there coming into our world down here" is meaningless to a secular age?[22] If this absent God is not known or experienced in our everyday life, as He surely is not, can any words about Him on Sunday mean something real to us or have any effect on our daily conduct? Clearly we are all secularized to a large degree, and just as evidently the biblical religion of both our fathers and current theologians is not "getting through" to the layman—who seems, nevertheless, to himself and his mates to be getting along pretty well. In this situation of a world "come of age," is it not better to prune Christian thought of its specifically religious content; at least of its supernatural, Godward references, so that we can say

[22] The reference here is to such works as the later writings of Dietrich Bonhoeffer, especially his *Letters and Papers from Prison* (E. Bethge, ed.; London: Fontana Books, 1963); William Hamilton, *op. cit.*; Bishop J. A. T. Robinson's *Honest to God* (Philadelphia: Westminster Press, 1963); and Paul Van Buren's *The Secular Meaning of the Gospel* (New York: The Macmillan Co., 1963); mention might also be made of the relevant, but less directly associated, writings of Rudolf Bultmann and Paul Tillich.

something meaningful and effective in a successful secular
period? Let us then (so the proposal concludes) cease to bemoan
the power of the world over the church and stop trying to
protect the church or its thought from the world. For history
shows that, in fact, the sharp contrast or distinction between the
two has only made the church self-righteous, dogmatic, anachronistic, and futile. What has just been called the weakness of the
denomination is precisely its strength and hope: namely, that
it *is* vulnerable to the world's influence, and as a result its holy,
separated elements are gradually slipping from its life!

What can we say to this proposal, especially after admitting
the very beneficial influences of culture on the church? And
what is the effect of this admission on the theme of our inquiry
as to how the church in our day can serve the world without
losing itself to the world? While a discussion of the needs of
theology in a secular age is plainly out of place here (since this
is not a book on theology), still something further can and
should be said on the subject.

Whatever one's position with regard to theological language—
whether we seek to develop a "religionless gospel" without
reference to God; whether we translate the "God out there" into
another, more secular view of the divine; or whether we merely
refrain from speaking of God's power and eternity—in all these
cases there still remains a core or essence of the gospel that is, in
the terms I seek to use in this volume, holy and transcendent. At
the least, this much-reduced and secularized gospel will proclaim the lordship of Jesus over the lives of those who call themselves Christian. That claim will, moreover, involve for those
who heed it an acceptance of powerlessness, a willingness to
sacrifice their own interests, a "being available for others," whoever they are, that is anything but worldly. Such an incarnation
of forgetfulness of self and of love for one's fellows is, in our
day as in that of our Lord, in striking contrast to anything the
world claims or encourages in a man. If every supernatural word
were deleted from our Gospels, such a proclamation and any
community built around it would still stand in glaring opposition
to the ordinary customs and conventions of society. For the
transcendent and the holy are far more apparent in a transformed
existence than in any system of petrified dogmas; and, as our

contemporary racial struggles so well illustrate, an ethical concern that accepts and rescues the "unacceptable" in society is far more of a threat to the established order than any amount of orthodox preaching. The contrast between church and world, between gospel or Word of God and our secular life, remains then as strong in these "secularized" theologies as in any others; as they themselves remind us, they have merely shifted the tension to a more central point, from the area of supernatural words to that of transformed lives. Whether these latter can remain intelligible and fruitful without a theological language to match and express this "transcendence," is a subject for another sort of book. Meanwhile it is agreed that the holy in the church—that which must be preserved against the world—is no particular brand of theology, form of liturgy, or even code of ethics. It is the presence of the claim of its Lord on the total existence of a community, and in response, the surrender and commitment of that community to Him in its thought, behavior, and common life. *This* form of the holy, more than anything else, seems to be absent from our current denominational life.

As many students of the church know, there is in our time a widespread feeling of frustration and emptiness with regard to both the ministry and the church in the forms in which we know them. The sociological changes I have described have (as Winter and Berger have so eloquently said) imprisoned the local churches in the residential confines of the middle classes; and these changes, combined with the secularization of our life, have stripped the church of much of the sense of holiness—that is, of both transcendence and relevance to the world—inherent in Christianity in its creative periods. This has led many scholars and not a few ministers to wonder if the local church, with its empty liturgy, its endless activities, its closed fellowship and overwhelming concern with personal "pastoral" problems, is a possible vehicle for the gospel in our technological and urban age—let alone for the works of responsible love which are surely called forth from any genuinely Christian community. There is so clearly a need for a ministry of reconciliation and of reform to areas and issues untouched by, and seemingly closed to, the local residential church—the labor unions, the inner city, the slums and tenements, racial problems, and so on—that it may well seem that the congregational community of Word and Sacrament, which has been the classical form for the church, is now irrelevant, too captive to its own smug residential milieu to spread the gospel or live it out in human reality.

While this criticism of the local churches and the seminaries that have fed them is valid, and is reflected throughout this book, one can give it only a qualified assent. It is certainly true that the development of an urban culture from which the residential areas are removed has shut off the local church, which is settled outside the great problem areas of our cities, from many of the tasks of ministry of the church as a whole. Other types of ministry than those serving local residential churches of the classic sort must therefore be developed; ministries to unions, to tenement districts, to areas of racial tension, and so on are clearly called for. Much as in the Roman Catholic Church, Protestantism must develop a multifaceted life, only part of which is involved in local church work. This will require some radical rethinking of the nature of the church and the ministry, especially for denominations of free-church traditions, since for them the church is almost by definition the local congregation. This freedom to recognize the new social situation that confronts us, and so to rethink our organizational forms, is what I am calling for in this book; and these new types of ministry, embodied in part in inner-city parishes, must be developed if the Christian faith is to be mediated to our world as a whole. It is certain that the total mission of the church to today's urban and technological world cannot be channeled through the local congregation and its ministry, and therefore the creation of new concepts of ministry is desperately needed.

This does not mean, however, that what we call the congregation, or the local church, does not and will not remain the center and seedbed of these other ministries. Were Christianity simply an ethical program, a series of reforms to be enacted and acts of mercy to be done, the local church might be replaced by other forms of ministry, freer to work in areas of suffering, tension, and conflict. Christian faith certainly involves such relevance to the world, such concern for its ills and suffering, and therefore the church in its ministry must reflect and act upon that concern.

Nevertheless, Christianity also concerns the inner nurture of men so that this sort of action may be its fruit; it is concerned with what a man believes and trusts, what he worships and adores, as well as what he does. Or, to paraphrase Luther's famous statement: "If love does the deeds (of mercy), then faith (a man's inner attitude, perspective, commitment) is the doer of those deeds." This correlation of inner trust or commitment with outer life and action is the center of Christian faith as here understood, expressed by our Lord in the conjunction of the two commandments to love both God and the neighbor, and by the importance throughout Christian history of both faith and works. It is expressed in the need for the Word and worship of God if a community of persons are to love one another, and in the interrelation of transcendence and relevance which is a major theme in this book. Thus "religion," taken as referring to that inner relation of repentance, trust, and obedience to God, is not antithetical to, but the foundation of, "true worldliness" in the sense of acts of mercy and love to the world around. As I shall argue here, a faith that is *not* thus outwardly relevant to the world's life has no genuine religious element of holiness or transcendence left within it; and correspondingly, without such inner faith in God, acts of love are in the long run not really possible in the world's life. The ministry of the church must maintain its concern with "religion," with the relation of man to God, if it is also to be concerned creatively with the world and with love of the human life around it. This concern with God, with His claim on us, with His judgment of us and His freeing love and mercy toward us, must remain the nuclear center of the church's life in order to make possible the community of love and the acts of reconciliation it offers to the world. The varied ministries of service depend in turn upon the fundamental ministry of Word and Sacrament, and on the inward relation of men to God in the worshiping congregation. In this book we shall consider the problems that at present beset the congregations of our land and their preaching and pastoral ministry, for through their renewal alone can the whole church become a fit instrument of the divine will.

2

The Historical Background

In the preceding pages I have tried to locate the center of the problem of the church and the world in our American church life. We found that the denomination, a form I have defined as the sect-type in Christendom, made the church unusually vulnerable to the domination of a secular culture and thus barely able to be the church, that is, a community able to mediate the holiness of God to the world. Our purpose in this chapter is to explore some of the various forces and influences that have created this situation, and to outline the two answers that, roughly speaking, American Christianity has given to this problem. Needless to say, there are innumerable factors, social, economic, and political as well as religious, that have influenced the development of sects into denominations and have given the sectarian form of the church the dominance it has had in American life. Among the most widely recognized of these factors are the frontier, the dominance of Anglo-Saxon groups, an expanding economic situation, the innate egalitarian democracy of the American scene, and so on. I should like to mention two intellectual elements which seem to me particularly illuminating: the Enlightenment and evangelical Christianity.

The first and most generally influential aspect of the Enlightenment on American church life was its optimistic and "secular" view of human society. For the Enlightenment the entire cosmos, and so also that small part of it which is human society, is formed and structured by rational laws.[1] Built into society in its political, economic, and social aspects are certain natural laws and structures to which a healthy community is obedient and which make society by nature harmonious, if they are obeyed. In politics these are the "natural rights of man"; in economics they are the laws of the free market; and in social relations they are the democratic ideals of the value of the individual and his self-development and self-realization. To the Enlightenment, therefore, these natural structures of society are "good"—God-given at Creation, if you are pious. Thus society is not in its essential nature a realm of evil or of sin, as was previously felt,[2] but a co-operative, harmonious place, a fit place for a constructive, valuable, and innocent existence based on the laws of creation and nature. Since, moreover, society is formed according to natural and therefore secular rules, to participate in it you do not need to be a Christian or a Jew, Baptist or Catholic. A society made up of a variety of religious groups became possible because by the Enlightenment society was considered to be natural and secular.

Now this view of society meant that a Christian, even a sectarian Christian, could participate in American life without feeling that he was compromising his Christianity. Under this influence the image of the world shifted from that of an evil place to that of a good place. Under the Enlightenment only the

[1] For excellent discussions of the Enlightenment, see J. H. Randall, Jr., *The Making of the Modern Mind* (Cambridge, Mass.: Houghton Mifflin Co., 1940), Chap. XI-XV; Ernest Cassirer, *The Philosophy of the Enlightenment* (Boston: Beacon Press, 1955); and Basil Willey, *The Seventeenth Century Background* (Garden City, N.Y.: Doubleday Anchor, 1953) and *The Eighteenth Century Background* (London: Chatto & Windus, 1950).

[2] For an illuminating description of this shift in the assessment of natural existence as "fallen," and so as a consequence of society as "evil," to one of society as good, cf. Willey's *Seventeenth Century Background*, Chap. II. Willey rightly credits this shift to the gradual emergence of humanism and of science in the late fifteenth, sixteenth, and seventeenth centuries among the intelligentsia; but it did not become really the common property of the majority of educated Western man until the full-blown Enlightenment of the eighteenth century.

vices of the world—not the essential structures of society—
were regarded as evil. And thus the social dimensions of the
Christian ethic in its sectarian form were removed by the
Enlightenment view of society.[3] For participation in the recognized vocations of society now came under secular standards of
lawfulness and citizenship and not the religious standard of
holiness, and if carried on according to the standards of citizenship it involved no compromise with that holiness. Thus the
sectarian American could now become a Democrat or Republican
in politics; a banker, laborer, even a policeman or soldier by
vocation, on the basis of the natural law of American society;
and this involved—because it was a secular vocation in a naturally
good society—no opposition to his Christian faith, nor did these
vocations compromise his Christian virtue. Ironically, therefore,
the saying familiar in conservative Protestantism that "politics is
politics and religion is religion," is largely derived from this
separation of religion and society in the views of the Enlightenment, though our fundamentalist friends do not realize it.[4]

[3] In this thesis there is, of course, some modification of H. Richard
Niebuhr's familiar theme that the difference between "sectarian ethics" and,
say, those of the eighteenth-century Methodists, in many other respects
similar, lay in the class origins of the leaders of this latter group: ". . . the
Methodist movement remained throughout its history in the control of men
who had been born and bred in the middle class and who were impressed
not so much by the social evils from which the poor suffered as by the
vices to which they succumbed." *Social Sources of Denominationalism*
(Hamden, Conn.: Shoe String Press, 1954), p. 67. While not questioning
for a moment the truth of the above insight, I should like to propose that
it is not insignificant that most semisectarian movements in the Enlightenment and post-Enlightenment world of the eighteenth and nineteenth centuries (cf. the Disciples, the Nazarenes, the Mormons, at least in the latter
days; the Pentecostal churches, etc.) have had the same nonsocial, personally centered, anti-vice ethical structure despite the clearly lower-class
origins of many of these groups. This suggests at the least that one effective
factor in the situation is the new view of social structures as "normal,"
"innocent," and therefore good, which the Enlightenment brought and
which has apparently been accepted by most modern "sects" (Jehovah's
Witnesses, of course, excepted). The Enlightenment provided for the
sectarian mind, therefore, what Calvin's ethic a hundred years earlier had
been for the middle classes, namely "a great unified conception which enabled the Christian to be active in the world with a good conscience and
without a break between a Christian ethical and the worldly ideals."
Wuensch, *Evangelische Wirtschaftslehre*, p. 339, quoted *ibid.*, p. 97.

[4] However capitalistic it may have appeared to be later, even Calvinism
in its beginnings rejected the modern dictum that the economic and po-

Most important, the general rules and standards that determine a man's day-to-day existence were now grounded in cultural standards and not religious ones. Henceforth a churchman acted in business, politics, and in the wider community generally according to the accepted standards of secular American life—whether those standards reflected common bourgeois virtues, the customs of the Southern way of life, or the requirements of nationalistic Americanism—and not according to biblical law or a denominational mode of existence. Thus under the influence of the Enlightenment the day-to-day existence of common churchgoing Americans became dominated by the natural and secular patterns of American communal life, and because of this influence we now participate in the economic and political structures of our society with few sectarian twinges of conscience.

Second, the Enlightenment emphasized man's freedom from authority,[5] the goodness and wisdom of the common man, and, as a consequence, the democratic process. These anti-authoritarian tendencies are the foundation of our peculiarly American political and social life in so far as it is genuinely democratic.

---

litical orders of society should be free from the control and interference of religious standards and authorities. On the contrary, both in theory and in practice it insisted that men's behavior in the courthouse and the market place be carried on according to the law of God, as found in God's Word and so as interpreted by church authorities. "The principle on which the collectivism of Geneva rested may be described as that of the omnicompetent church. The religious community formed a closely organized society, which, while using the secular authorities as police officers to enforce its mandates, not only instructed them as to the policy to be pursued, but was itself a kind of state, prescribing by its own legislation the standard of conduct to be used by its members, putting down offenses against public order and public morals, providing for the education of youth and for the relief of the poor . . . In the sixteenth century, whatever the political condition, the claim of the Calvinist churches is everywhere to exercise a collective responsibility for the moral conduct of their members in all the various relations of life, and to do so, not least, in the sphere of economic transactions, which offer peculiarly insidious temptations to lapses to immorality." R. H. Tawney, *Religion and the Rise of Capitalism* (Middlesex, Eng.: Penguin Books, 1948), pp. 132-33.

[5] Cf. Kant's definition of the Enlightenment: "Enlightenment is man's exodus from his self-incurred tutelage. Tutelage is the inability to use one's understanding without the guidance of another person . . . 'dare to know' . . . Have the courage to use your own understanding; this is the motto of the Enlightenment." Immanuel Kant, "Beantwortung der Frage: Was ist Aufklärung?" quoted in Cassirer, *op. cit.*, p. 163.

The sects in their own way had emphasized both these basic affirmations: here, too, there was lay control of church life and no ecclesiastical authority. Thus sect and Enlightenment joined hands to create our democratically structured denominational church; and thus in its formative period the most influential force in American culture, the Enlightenment, pushed American religion in the direction of a lay-centered, sectarian understanding of the church rather than any other. The American denomination, a nonhierarchical, nonauthoritarian, nontheological, nonsacramental, voluntary, free and equal association of men in religion, is the result both of the Enlightenment and of sectarian influences.

This movement into a society where the Enlightenment held sway—a society that was secularly determined and governed—received an important "assist" from evangelical Christianity. Dominant in the nineteenth century through the many revivals that swept the country, evangelical Christianity provided the religious content for much of American Protestantism as it moved, under Enlightenment influences, from sectarian separation into an amalgamation with American culture. Evangelical Christianity has, of course, many facets: for our purposes its concentration on personal character and the ultimate destiny of the individual human soul were particularly important. This soul, sunk in sin (as the gospel hymns vividly relate), has been rescued by Jesus from damnation. Having accepted Him in a vivid personal experience of salvation, this soul may now walk in personal security with Him and thus, through both faith and righteousness, be led by Him to its glorious reward in heaven. Almost universal in the nineteenth century, this "gospel" Christianity was the American form of pietism, since it was a religion of inward feeling and personal holiness, whose goal was purely that of individual salvation in the next life.

While there is no question that its emphasis on personal salvation through God's forgiving love enshrines the center of the gospel, on the whole this evangelical understanding of Christianity had no relevance to the cultural and historical life within which Christian men must live. Its "heresy," if it may be said to have one, was that it omitted God the Father, the Creator, .

Preserver, and Ruler of all human history and of every human community, in favor of Jesus the Son, who is related exclusively to individual souls and their destinies. Thus while evangelical Christianity concerned itself relentlessly with issues of personal vice—and so prepared a man to be a *respectable* member of the community—it had relatively little to say about his Christian obligations to be a responsible member of society.[6] It tended to overlook such moral issues as those involved in the accumulation of personal property, in social institutions such as slavery and later segregation, or in the use of violence either in a war or in the exercise of government. Quite unlike sectarian Christianity, therefore, it involved for its adherents no separation from the world, for it required little change in a man's social patterns of behavior as entrepreneur, soldier, or citizen. Like the medieval Catholic layman, the believer in "gospel Christianity" could go on about his business in the world unaffected by the Christian standards he professed—although he had to conduct his business or his politics "purely," that is, without indulging in personal vice or allowing smoking on his factory property or the sale of alcohol in the town he lived in. Alike typical figures in this era were Southern slave-owners and Yankee slave ship captains, who read their Bibles daily and would have felt it a dangerous compromise to their Christian principles to do business about their slaves on Sunday or let alcohol touch their lips.

Despite this vast difference in ethics from the sectarian type, evangelical Christianity had many elements in common with it. Being "inward" or "personal" forms of Christianity, both were

[6] These remarks on the social implications of evangelical Christianity run, of course, counter to the thesis of Timothy Smith's remarkable book *Revivalism and Social Reform* (Nashville, Tenn.: Abingdon Press, 1957), especially Chaps. X-XIV. While there is no denying the evidence he marshals there, it seems none the less true that any social effects "gospel Christianity" may have had were more peripheral than central, more infrequent than frequent; and that the main conscious thrust of revivalist ethics was as I have described it, toward issues of personal vice rather than those of social structure and policy. In this it differed from the liberal social gospel which with deliberate and almost exclusive emphasis concentrated its religious force on social problems. Certainly the long-term emphasis of evangelical Christianity, its general character as revealed since the 1850's and 1860's and in its present character among Southern and Midwestern conservative groups, has been (as here described) to concentrate on a personal ethic or holiness rather than on the social and communal obligations of love.

anti-ecclesiastical, nonsacramental, and nonliturgical; both felt
only danger to religion in the authority of a priesthood; and
neither saw much value in the theological or scholarly tasks of
the church. As did the sects, the evangelicals therefore rejected
all those elements of objective holiness so emphasized by the
church-type (a holy priesthood, sacrament, dogma, and monastic
perfection), in their concentration on personal belief and personal holiness.[7] Thus evangelical Christianity provided just the
understanding of religion needed by erstwhile sectarian traditions when, under the influence of the Enlightenment, they shed
their separatist tendencies and sought to join an expanding common American culture. The inward and ethical religion of the
sects, pruned now of those social implications that had required
a sociological separation, became the individualistic gospel of
evangelicalism, controlling a man's behavior in the area of personal
vice but allowing him complete freedom to participate in the
public life of the economic, political, and social environment.
Much of recent American Protestantism, then, has resulted from
the amalgamation of these three elements: a sectarian understanding of the forms of church life and polity; accepting
participation in the world through the Enlightenment understanding of society; and finding the content, ethical standards,
goals, and limits of its religion in the evangelical piety of personal
holiness and individual salvation. When these three elements had
united, the result was the conservative denominational form of
the church, still predominant in the South and the rural Midwest. To its general structure and problems we shall now turn.[8]

[7] Cf. the chapter on the influence of evangelicalism on American religion,
ibid., Chap. V. These influences Smith lists as follows: "The traditional
predominance of the clergy in the spiritual and organizational work of the
churches now gave place rapidly to the enthusiastic expression of lay participation and control. The spirit of interdenominational brotherhood . . .
came swiftly to maturity . . . Ethical concerns replaced dogmatic zeal in
evangelical preaching and writing. And, equally important, Arminian views
crowded out Calvinism in much of the dogma that remained." *Ibid.*, p. 80.

[8] In one of his perceptive articles on American church history, Sydney
Mead has characterized this later nineteenth-century amalgam of evangelicalism and Enlightenment as follows: "What was not so obvious at the
time was that the United States, in effect, had two religions, or at least two
different forms of the same religion, and that the prevailing Protestant
ideology represented a syncretistic mingling of the two. The first was
the religion of the denominations, which was commonly articulated in the

I am picturing here conservative Protestant religion *in* culture. Although sectarian in its polity and understanding of the church, it is now very much a part of the community: respected, popular, and successful. In the rural Midwest and all over the South it forms the sole area of Protestant Christendom remaining in Western society, where—as Sunday traffic jams in Nashville prove—the city of the world attends, supports, and promotes the city of God.[9] Now this sociological movement toward "establishment" has inevitably had its effects on the character of the religion involved. As sectarian, evangelical Protestantism has moved into and become a part of culture—as Presbyterians and Episcopalians in the suburbs have been joined by Methodists, Baptists, and Disciples, and even by the Churches of Christ—so, inevitably, the religion of conservative Protestantism has developed steadily away from its originally pietistic form. While retaining certain nuclear elements of its sectarian and evangelical character, it has nevertheless taken on other not insignificant

terms of scholastic Protestant orthodoxy and almost universally practiced in terms of the experimental religion of pietistic revivalism . . . The second was the religion of the democratic society and the nation. This was rooted in the rationalism of the Enlightenment (to go no further back) and was articulated in terms of the destiny of America, under God, to be fulfilled by perfecting the democratic way of life for the example and betterment of all mankind. . . . This religion was almost universally practiced in terms of the burgeoning middle-class society and its 'free enterprise' system . . ." After mentioning the same compartmentalism and acceptance of the social ideals of its secular environment that we have noted, Mead sums up this description as follows: "But whatever historical explanations are accepted as most plausible, there remains the general agreement that, at the time Protestantism in America achieved its greatest dominance of the culture, it had also achieved an almost complete ideological and emotional identification with the burgeoning bourgeois society and its free-enterprise system, so that 'in 1876 Protestantism presented a massive, almost unbroken front in its defense of the social status quo' ". Sydney Mead, "From Denominationalism to Americanism," *Journal of Religion*, 36 (January, 1956), 2-6. (The quotation at the end of Mead's remarks is from Henry F. May, *Protestant Churches and Industrial America* [New York: Harper & Brothers, 1949], p. 91.).

[9] When in the spring of 1963 the writer and his wife were driving through Birmingham, Alabama, they were confronted with two signs unusually symbolic of this wedding of culture and religion. The first was a full-sized advertizing billboard showing steeples and happy couples, and proclaiming across the top: THE NICE PEOPLE OF BIRMINGHAM GO TO CHURCH. The second, seen just moments later as the traffic thickened toward the center of town, was a sign on a large car: VISITOR GO HOME.

church-type characteristics, although this has been absolutely
unintended and unknown to itself. Ironically, the similarity of
this deliberately unworldly and virulently anti-Catholic form of
Protestantism to medieval Catholic Thomism is in fact remarkable. It has become, as I often say to my students, a kind of
"poor man's Thomism." Let us look briefly at five areas where
church-type elements have begun to appear in the denominational life of conservative Protestantism.

Originally, as we have seen, sectarian and evangelical Christianity de-emphasized doctrinal orthodoxy in favor of personal
piety, and thus turned away from creeds and confessions as tests
of Christian faith. Recently, however, conservative Protestantism
has had to establish its own dogmas, "lists of fundamentals" or
"essentials" which must be believed if one would be counted a
man with real Christian faith. This change toward an external
doctrinal orthodoxy has become necessary because of the social
changes of these groups. Being now in the world, conservative
Christians find themselves related in schools, literature, and drama
to other, often conflicting, sorts of truth. This continual ex-
posure endangers their Christian faith unless Christian truth is
clearly defined in easily comprehensible and identifiable form—
i.e., in creeds and confessions—and rigidly held to. The sectarian
separation in communal existence, in behavior, and in the totality
of thought, which had made possible a relaxed view of creeds
and theology, has *in* the world led to separation from cultural
influence in the area only of strictly defined biblical dogmas. In
this separation, orthodoxy in the churches is, as in Catholicism,
completely removed from all relation to the science and philosophy of its day; it remains both untested and unchanged by
the world's ideas and standards, and is therefore believed on the
grounds of loyal faith alone. The recent reappearance of the
evolution controversy in Tennessee underlines these remarks.
Here we see one-time sectarian and evangelical groups, armed
with a biblical dogma, seeking to control—for all the world like
Pope Innocent the Third—the intellectual life of their society.

The Catholic double standard in ethics also appears universally
in this type of Protestantism. We mean by this the assumption,
common in contemporary Protestant churches in conservative
areas, that there is one standard of behavior for the clergyman,

who must not smoke, drink, or hear tales of the flesh, and another for the layman, who does so but feels he shouldn't (because his evangelical father did not), and therefore insists with fanatical severity that his minister should not. What has happened in this strange development is roughly the following. When it first shed its rigorous social ethic on moving into society, sectarian Christianity poured all its intense moral fervor into its abhorrence of the worldly vices. And while, as we saw, the good evangelical could become rich without a twinge, he could not drink, play a game on Sunday, or swear without fearing for his soul's salvation. His freedom from personal vice was made the only meaning of Christian perfection and the sole test of personal holiness. Later, however, as these same groups have moved upward from the lower to the upper middle classes, from shopkeepers to executives, from small towns to the suburbs, this concentration on personal vices has become increasingly uncomfortable and impractical. Now the layman who attends insurance conventions in New York and lives out his leisure hours in the country club and on suburban back-patios no longer wishes to apply these rigid and exceedingly dry standards to himself. Knowing, however, from his father's image that this *is* Christian perfection and so must be maintained *somewhere*, he heaps these demands on the poor sacrificial victim who has the role of minister in his church. Like Cyprian's ideal bishop, the modern minister alone bears all the holiness of our suburban congregations—a role as unprofitable for them as it is impossible for himself.[10] In other words, as these groups have moved

[10] Cyprian (bishop of Carthage in the years 249-58) viewed the bishop as absolutely necessary for the existence of the church, and so for the possibility of salvation; but he also felt that this unexpendable bishop must be personally holy and sinless, lest he cease to be a vehicle of grace and become instead a vehicle of contagion: "Nor let the people flatter themselves that they can be free from the contagion of sin, while communicating with a priest who is a sinner, and yielding their consent to the unjust and unlawful episcopacy of their overseer . . . all are bound to the sin who have been contaminated by the sacrifice of a profane and unrighteous priest . . . On which account a people obedient to the Lord's precepts, and fearing God, ought to separate themselves from a sinful prelate . . ." Cyprian, "Epistle 67," sec. 3, found in *The Ante-Nicene Fathers*, A. Roberts and J. Donaldson, eds., Vol. V (Grand Rapids, Mich.: Eerdmans, 1951), p. 370. Cf. also Epistle 63:4. Because no man is sinless, and a fortiori because no parishioner can be assured of his priest's sinlessness, this principle of priestly perfection

up in culture, the rigid sectarian, pietistic moral code has been softened for the culturated layman but maintained for the clergy. We might note that in both cases, as in medieval Catholicism, Christian obligation is understood in strictly legal terms, a Christian layman being a man who follows the natural customs of his community in his own life but disapproves of such activities for his minister, and a Christian clergyman being one who not only disapproves of such activities but also refrains from them.[11]

Two separated realms of ethics, familiar both to Thomism and to Lutheranism, also appear. For the modern churchman the world and its society is governed by natural law, in this case the bourgeois, nationalistic, and often racially inspired standards of the American scene. In this "downtown world" of everyday activities the layman and even the preacher obey the secular standards that rule over our commercial, legal, and social life, and it literally never occurs to the churchman (any more than to a good Catholic) that the standards of the gospel are relevant here.

---

proved unworkable and was overcome by Augustine in his argument with the Donatists from 395 to roughly 411 or 415. It is, said Augustine, the presence of Christ and Holy Spirit in the sacraments that makes them valid and efficacious, not the personal sanctity of the priest or bishop (cf. *De baptismo contra Donatistas*). Since that time the two-level ethic has, of course, remained in Catholicism, but the saving power of the church has long since ceased to depend upon the perfect saintliness of the clergy.

Examples of the newer Protestant two-level ethic abound in conservative church life. Sometimes the distinction in standard between clergy and laity is admitted, sometimes hypocritically overlooked—but in almost all suburban and urban situations it is there. The worst example this writer knows happened to a young Disciples of Christ graduate student at Vanderbilt who was temporary minister in a church near Nashville, Tennessee. The church was, by all appearances, satisfied with his work and his preaching, and had even indicated to him its willingness to pay him a slightly better salary. Then one Monday evening, while at supper at the chief elder's house, he was offered by the same elder a glass of sherry. Brought up in the less dryly conservative traditions of New Haven, Connecticut, he accepted with some surprise and delight, and the evening continued with all the usual Southern courtesy and charm. The next day, however, he was informed by the board that never again could he preach in that church. The rigid holiness ethic, relaxed now for laymen and elders, is nevertheless ruthlessly applied to the minister.

Every minister of a conservative Protestant congregation feels the crushing weight of this double standard, and many of them find it the most difficult and painful aspect of their ministry. The "holiness" of the Catholic priest, while partly personal and moral, rests rather with his office and its sacramental powers; in his person he can be normal and human, and, as

He accepts property and its unlimited accumulation; he accepts the use of force by the courts and other agencies of law enforcement; he accepts segregation, if that be the rule of his community; and he accepts the violence of war—all without any thought of compromise with his faith. For conservative Protestant as for medieval Catholic, the gospel has to do with personal vice and the problem of heaven, and so the gospel leaves completely out of its scope the wider community issues of politics, economics, and social relationships.[12] As in Catholic Thomism, social affairs are governed entirely by natural law, the gospel ethic being confined to matters that have to do with one's entrance into the next life—i.e., drinking, smoking, and gambling. When one recalls, moreover, that the layman now has very little intention of applying even these inhibitions to his own habits of personal life, one can see how weak the whole ethical structure of this once evangelical but now culturated conserva-

---

numerous army chaplains will witness, there is little gulf between his human person and those of his flock. The holiness of the Protestant pastor, on the other hand, is solely personal and moral, a quality of his character and life, not of his office. This created no gulf when the entire congregation was dedicated to the same goal, but throws up an insurmountable barrier in our modern situation, when laymen live by one standard and the minister by another. Then, as one pastor described it, "One never has any real contacts with anyone: laughter and jokes cease when one enters the room, normal conversation halts, everyone becomes pious and sincere, clean and selfless, in order now to commune in the holy realm of the minister—a realm in which none of them really exists except when they are with the preacher. Like a space suit, this unreality accompanies him everywhere he goes." Worst of all, of course, as most serious ministers agree, is what it does to the minister himself. For the role of "holy man" in the congregation is spiritually deadly: either he assumes that he fills the role adequately, and thus becomes impossible for anyone else to bear, or he knows that he does not fill it and is inwardly plunged into despair. In either case, the unpleasant unction and slight aura of falseness probably flow more directly from this aspect of the minister's role in modern life than from any other. What is needed is a good dose of Luther: "Therefore let us keep quiet about holiness and holy people. We know that those have been made holy who have become conscious sinners rather than unconscious sinners. They do not presume to have any righteousness of their own—for it is nonexistent . . . Thus they know themselves and God." "Psalm 51," commentary, *Luther's Works*, J. Pelikan, ed., Vol. 12 (St. Louis, Mo.: Concordia, 1955), p. 325. And secondly, there is needed a deep reexamination of the entire battery of standards, both for ministers and laity, that function in our present churches.

[11] A friend and colleague of the writer, the now deceased Rev. William

tive Protestantism has become. Guided in the week by his community's moral code, and applying what he regards as the "gospel ethic" only to his minister's life, the average layman is hard put to it to reply when asked: "What distinctive conduct on *your* part does your churchmanship require?" About all he can answer is "Giving of my time, energy, and substance to the activities of the church"—an excellent medieval "works" answer, but far from the anti-institutional bent of either his sectarian or his evangelical ancestors!

As in Catholicism, there develop "religious areas of life" separated from secular areas and sacred in their own right. The best examples from earlier times of these objectively sacred places and occasions are found, of course, in medieval Catholicism, where the works that supported church life, the property that belonged to the church, the clerical status of officials of the church, and even the festivals of the church were considered in themselves holy and therefore quite uncontaminated by the secular world around them. In each of these aspects of church life the worlds' methods, its goals, and even its standards could in fact dominate, as may be seen in the sharpness and ruthlessness of a good deal of Catholic practice in the Middle Ages. To the amazement of Protestant and especially sectarian critics, however, such "worldly" characteristics were not regarded by Catholics as contaminating these sacred areas. And now, ironically, the same strange situation of objectively holy entities (i.e., having no personal, inward religious content) in the midst of secular culture has appeared in Protestant life, especially con-

---

Kirkland, used to relate the story of his ordination in the Methodist Church. For this occasion he flew from his home in Poughkeepsie, New York, all the way to Nashville, Tennessee, and according to his telling of it was asked "not whether I loved the Lord Jesus at all, or even wished to serve him, but simply and solely whether I used tobacco."

[12] An illustration of the two-area ethic in an earlier stage of conservative American Protestantism may be found in the Southern Presbyterian interpretation, common in Civil War times, of the "spirituality of the Church." Dr. James Henley Thounwell argued that "if Christ is the head of the Church, then the Church in its organizational form must confine its work to that which Christ commissioned it to do. Christ did not commission it to run the state or reconstruct society afresh." Quoted in T. Watson Street, *The Story of Southern Presbyterians*, (Richmond, Va.: John Knox Press, 1960), p. 50.

servative Protestant life. First, of course, are the "works" of church life which, though perhaps quite secular in character— as, contracting for a new coat of paint on the church, organizing a billiard room in the church basement, or increasing the per capita contribution of members—are regarded as sacred not because of what is done, but simply because the activity takes place in or for the church. In the same way, the most blatant advertising and the most objectionable techniques of the "big sell" are common enough in evangelical and especially revivalist practices—as church advertisements in any paper in the South demonstrate—without apparently detracting in the slightest from the religious character of the occasion or its message. Moving a little further afield, we see religious publishing houses, though normally in business for profit, claiming tax exemption on the grounds of the holiness of their subject matter, or more accurately, their ownership—as do the parking spaces for the many religious enterprises in Nashville. One cannot help but be reminded of the immense tracts of medieval land which were tax-free because their proprietorship happened to be clerical. An "all-day gospel hymn sing" in a Southern town has every bit of the atmosphere of a medieval festival, in which there is a good deal of ordinary down-to-earth fun combined with this objectively "religious" or holy occasion. On records and radio, moreover, gospel songs can be interspersed amidst the most banal and sensual popular music without any feeling that these songs, or the religiosity of the singer, are thereby contaminated. And finally, at the beginning of all public festivals in the South, such as college football games, the conservative Protestant prayer takes its place alongside the Catholic prayer in our Northern cities as the necessary sanctification of what is otherwise a completely secular occasion. As in Catholicism, therefore, an objective realm of the sacred has appeared within the life of the culture, a development so utterly foreign to the sectarian origin of these same groups as to be vastly ironical.

The last and most significant "church-type" characteristic in modern conservative Protestantism is its astonishing emphasis on the visible church, that is, on the organization, growth, and successful operation of the church as an institution. Among the groups least hierarchical and most anti-institutional in their past history, this organizational emphasis is at present the greatest. For example, issues of biblical truth or moral righteousness—supposedly important in themselves to evangelical churches—are often now quite frankly settled, not on the basis of truth or moral content, but of their effect upon the stability and growth of the organization of the church. The recent Southern Baptist debate on the interpretation of Scripture and the right of the individual to his own view, a right hallowed in Baptist history, was judged solely on organizational grounds: "The book was controversial, and will cause dissension in the convention."[13] In most evangelical churches, many of them Methodist and Disciples as well as Baptist, the issue of race cannot be raised in the church because, as is frankly admitted, it might "split the church" or "controversy unsettles a growing operation." Thus loyalty to the organization—what the Catholics used to refer to in terms of the traditional virtues of charity, obedience, and unity[14]—has become the central obligation of modern conservative ministers

[13] The reference here is, of course, to the recent expulsion of Prof. Ralph Elliott from Midwestern Baptist Theological Seminary. The writer attended a meeting at Vanderbilt at which the then president of the Southern Baptist Convention, the Rev. Mr. Hobbs, defended the expulsion in the terms asserted in the text. Admitting freely that many other Baptist professors held the views expressed in the book, that they were in fact fairly conservative views, and that the book dealt with materials regularly taught in other Southern Baptist seminaries, Hobbs nevertheless insisted that the expulsion, "a purely administrative matter," was justified because of the controversy the book had caused among Baptists, and because Elliott (to his credit, one must think) had refused voluntarily to withdraw the book from further publication because of the controversy. For a denomination which centers its official theory concerning itself about the concept of "man's freedom of conscience against all authority," this subordination of individual interpretations of Scripture and of the controversies that inevitably arise therefrom to the purely church-type values of stability and peace would be humorous were it not so tragic.

[14] The principle that love for the unity of the Body of Christ—i.e., the stability and harmony of the church as a whole—is the most direct form of love or *caritas*, and so the clearest evidence of the Holy Spirit and the highest Christian virtue, is classically expressed by Augustine: "Those who take or cause offense are those who are offended in Christ and his Church. If you keep hold of charity, you will take offense neither in Christ nor in the Church; and you will desert neither Christ nor the Church. The deserter of the Church (even if it be impure) cannot be in Christ, since he is not among Christ's members . . . for the lover of his brother endures all things for unity's sake. In the unity of charity brotherly love consists." "First Homily on I John," sec. 12, found in *Augustine's Later Works*, John Burnaby, ed., Library of Christian Classics, Vol. VIII (Philadelphia: Westminster Press, 1955), p. 268. "On what is anyone to ground assurance that

and laymen, replacing the older, typical sectarian obligations both to the truth of the gospel and to the ethic of holiness. Church-type organizationalism has thus joined hands with our commercial culture's innate corporate consciousness to weaken almost fatally those very conservative elements of holiness that expanding groups such as the Baptists claim to be preserving against culture!

These, then, are some of the facets of church-type life which have begun to appear in Protestantism as it has gradually become established within culture. One might note as a humorous aside the reappearance of honorific titles of culture applied to the clergy in many erstwhile sectarian church groups. Because such titles as "Your Grace" and "Your Holiness" implied both religious sanctity and social prestige, most sectarian groups in their early days did not allow their preachers to be addressed in any special way, even as "the Reverend Mr. Smith," fearing this might set him in some way apart from and above the congregation. Now that we have joined the world again, however, ranks and titles have once more taken on importance for us, and having in our past already dispensed with the available clerical tags, our denominational clergy are left groping somewhat frantically after academic ones. Thus in no Baptist, Disciples, or even Methodist clerical meeting—groups which have always distrusted theological education—can any man safely fail to call another man "doctor," whether the title has an academic origin or not. At a Baptist theological conference several years ago the humorous chairman, the Rev. Mr. Dahlberg, suggested that to save embarrassment "everybody assume what everybody already hoped, and address every one else as 'doctor' for the duration of the conference."

The differences from normative Catholicism remain, of course,

---

he has received the Holy Spirit? Let him inquire of his own heart: if he loves his brother, the Spirit of God abides in him . . . let him see if there is in him the love of peace and unity, love of the church that is spread throughout the world . . . all of us are in one body, and have one Head in heaven." "Sixth Homily on I John," sec. 10, *ibid.*, p. 308. This moving identity of love for the brethren with the unity of Christ's church has had its unfortunate implications, as Roman Catholic history and our own Baptist example show; ironically, however, when somewhat differently interpreted, the same identity of Christian love and unity lies at the heart of contemporary ecumenical endeavor.

immense. There is no sacred ecclesiastical hierarchy, nor are there any holy sacraments here. The locus of the holy—what is not cultural—is in conservative Protestantism found elsewhere than in Catholicism: first, in biblical doctrine, which nothing can question; second, in the vivid emotional experience of salvation, which every believer should experience; and third, in the moral code of personal freedom from vice. These differences from Catholicism, however, do not tend in our day to strengthen this form of religion. In the end conservative Protestantism has become in fact more vulnerable to culture than its Catholic counterpart, and if anything no more genuinely a creative form of Christian life. For these first two areas or elements of its life that are separated and holy, namely, the biblical doctrine and the emotional experience of salvation, are in their present forms religiously uncreative and ultimately at the mercy of the culture which this form of Protestantism has already embraced.

Briefly put, the biblical doctrines so rigorously defended as holy are kept quite out of relation to the thought world of culture and so of the laity in the churches, with the result that they remain unintelligible, abstract, and irrelevant—and thus quite ineffective for their lives. Correspondingly, the social and intellectual changes these groups have undergone have made the older evangelical experience of salvation impossible for them, with the result that the holy decisions and revivals of older days have become a mere empty formality with no holy content at all. Thus has conservative Protestantism become barren, because two of its separated elements have ceased to be creative media of the holy; and conservative Protestantism itself has thus, in turn, become increasingly vulnerable to amalgamation with culture.[15]

It is above all on the ethical level that this amalgamation is most apparent. The two-level ethic, distinguishing clergy from laity, has made it possible for the layman (but not the minister) to live merely according to the social standards of his society. Freely he smokes, drinks, goes to shows, plays golf on Sunday afternoon, and so on. I do not mean to imply that these are bad things in themselves, but certainly no one will deny that they are cultural, or that in permitting himself these pleasures the layman

[15] A fuller discussion of these two problems, of doctrine and of worship, will be forthcoming in Chaps. IV and V below.

is obeying a secular rather than a religious standard. The two-area ethic, distinguishing social and political issues from "Christian" moral issues, means that in their political, social, and economic behavior the people of the churches are totally governed by the customs and mores of their community. The layman is therefore bewildered if from the church he hears any challenge of these cultural ways. As a leading Methodist layman in Alabama said recently, "We don't want to leave the Methodist Church, but we will have to if they continue with this racial integration stuff." It is simply not the business of the church to deal with issues beyond those of personal vice, and even there its authority is *now* dubious in the minds of the laity. Clearly the church here has lost all its power and authority in the society of men.[16] Filled as it is with the world, promoted by the important forces of the world, it seems unable to effect any transformation of that world or even of itself. Since its directing members live in society and rule both

[16] An article in the the *New Orleans Times-Picayune* for March 21, 1963, told of a "rump" organization of Methodist ministers and laymen sponsored by the "Mississippi Association of Methodist Ministers and Laymen." Meeting in Jackson, Mississippi, this group resolved to place "segregationist" and "conservative" churchmen in important church posts "to prevent a change in racial customs." A new twist was given to sectarian separation from the world when one speaker, according to the article, suggested secession if the control of the Methodist Church does not remain conservative: "We must heed the injunction, 'Come out from among them and be separate, saith the Lord.'" A calmer voice apparently urged, however, that "as long as the separate [Negro] jurisdiction is maintained, I think we should continue to support our Church." The same speaker charged that they (the ministers) "have busied themselves so mightily in political matters, social matters, economic matters, that they have neglected the saving of souls and the Gospel of Christ." The meeting ended vowing support for any "conservative" against any "liberal," pledging support to the segregated organizational structure of the church; they also contended that integration of races is not commanded by God nor taught by Christ; and they expressed their full opposition to the "concept of one world, one church, one race." All this illustrates our thesis that (1) there is a two-area ethic in the contemporary conservative Protestant Church, and (2) the authority of the church is by no means felt to be binding on his ethical decisions by the average churchman. To be fair to the Methodist Church in Mississippi and Alabama, however, it should also be said that many of its ministers have spoken out clearly on this issue, twenty-eight of them having signed a very forthright statement on racial problems and the churches. Furthermore, while the majority of local churches are both silent and inactive, still, as far as the writer's experience is concerned, the only organized struggle against segregation and segregationist ideas among the whites of Alabama and Mississippi is carried on by the church in other aspects of its total work,

society and the church, the latter is in danger of capitulating completely to the status quo. For it lives on that status quo, and still has no basis for criticizing it. More than Catholicism, which, as the experience of school integration in New Orleans indicates, at least defends a rational natural law critical of *evil* social customs and holds up a monastic ideal critical of *all* social customs, this sort of Protestantism is not only in but also *of* the world. This tendency to fit into the status quo has only increased as conservative congregations have become more and more identical with the successful upper middle class and their churches have progressively moved to the suburbs. There they function largely as Sunday suburban fellowships, devoted mostly to the problems of the suburb—family and personal—and not to the problems of "downtown," where the men work and live and think, and where the social structures of life are determined.[17] Conservative Protestantism in America still appears to be strong, for in the South

---

such as the Westminster Fellowships, the youth groups of various kinds, church-related colleges, and the like. Despite the inability of the local church to deal with this problem, the church as a whole has done much in racial matters, and in the Deep South has been, among whites, the only consistent force against segregation.

The apparent willingness of modern laymen to leave their churches whenever they offend one or more of their cherished secular values may be poignantly compared with the fear and horror felt by earlier Christians at having deserted the church under threat of torture or death in times of persecution. For example, in the Decian persecution of 250 A.D. many Christians had become *lapsi*—those who made sacrifice at Roman order; later, when the persecution receded, they begged, cajoled, and almost forced their way back into the church, so awful was it to them to be banished therefrom—even under pain of death. Cyprian, the bishop of Carthage, wrote of them, "Who could be so callous, so stony-hearted, who so unmindful of brotherly love, as to remain dry-eyed in the presence of so many of his own kin who are broken now, shadows of their former selves, dishevelled, in the trappings of grief?" *The Lapsed*, trans. and annot. by Maurice Bévenot, S.J., sec. 4, found in *Ancient Christian Writers*, Vol. 25 (Westminster, Md.: The Newman Press, 1957), p. 16. One feels that this description of pitiful supplicants would hardly fit those dissident laymen who now propose to leave the church! Apparently, while Christians in the year 250 believed that the church declared the truth about reality, so that desertion was really serious, no such feeling of the *truth* of the Christian understanding of existence now holds, with the result that one can defy it at will and without fear. See Chap. IV for a further discussion of this problem.

[17] For a fascinating and authoritative study of this issue, cf. Gibson Winter's *The Suburban Captivity of the Churches* (Garden City, N.Y.: Doubleday & Co., 1961), esp. Chaps. 2, 3, and 4.

and the rural Midwest it remains one of the really dominant forces in culture. But its own fundamental religious structure is weak. It is in culture, but has little means of defense against culture, and those significant elements in its life which in the past have borne the holy are today quite unable to maintain this transcendence of society, and almost unable to maintain themselves.

The other major resolution of the problem of the church and culture is the liberal church, characteristic largely of our Northern urban life, but increasingly common in urban life everywhere. With the same ultimate roots in the sectarian form of the church and in the Enlightenment, it has taken other elements of their life and used them in a new way to form a synthesis quite different from the conservative. From the Enlightenment liberalism took its high estimate of scientific method and its positive and optimistic evaluation of human culture. But instead of placing these elements as an independent layer of life *below* the biblical gospel and evangelical religion, as did conservatism, liberalism reinterpreted Christianity, its gospel, and its ethic in their terms and thus made Christianity into the religious expression of this developing scientific and humanitarian culture.

One might say that the main difference between liberal and conservative churches—say, between the Disciples and the Churches of Christ, or between different groups in the Southern Baptist Convention—is not that the one affirms and capitulates to modern culture while the other rejects it. Rather the difference lies in the way the two deal with the culture they *both* accept— for they drive the same Chevrolets, go to the same doctors, stare at the same TV sets, run the same businesses, are protected by the same missiles, and afraid of the same sputniks. But while the conservative groups let this culture dominate their life six days a week and allow it no truck with their religion on Sunday, liberals have sought to think out their religion in the same terms as they thought out everything else. Neither solution is perfect, but surely the latter is more honest and creative—since (as, ironically, the sects have always insisted) a religion unrelated to a man's *existence* in his day-to-day life has little relevance, and therefore no transcendent, saving power.

Conceived in the enthusiasm of the Enlightenment for the goodness and order of culture, liberalism saw Christianity as the highest
development of a culture that was steadily progressing. Thus the
truth of Christianity was in accord with and could be determined
by the latest cultural criteria of science, in which the Enlightenment so much believed. Since religious truth was based, not on
a supernatural revelation transcendent to man's reason, but on
human religious experience, it could, like any other form of
experience, be tested by the cultural norms of scientific method,
empirical philosophy, and the highest developments of conscience.[18] Worship was understood in correspondingly cultural
terms: the sermon became an ethical or philosophical exhortation
addressed to the educated laity in the pews, and the goal of worship was a rededication of enlightened participants to Christian
and moral ideals. For the clear purpose of Christianity was not to
save souls for heaven, but to inspire Christian citizens for moral
service in human society. The Christian ethic was now related
entirely to cultural and social needs: the idea of the Kingdom of
God transformed itself from the concept of an apocalyptic and

[18] Auguste Sabatier (1839-1901) represents a very clear and quite typical
liberal position with regard to Christian truth and the norms by which it
should be tested: "The principle of criticism of Christian dogmas can only
be the principle of Christianity itself, which is anterior to all dogmas, and
which it is the aim of dogmas to manifest and apply. Now the principle
of Christianity is not a theoretical doctrine: it is religious experience—the
experience of Christ and his disciples through the centuries." A. Sabatier,
Outlines of a Philosophy of Religion (London: Hodder and Stoughton,
1906), p. 267. Because of the immanence of God in man and their continuity one with another, Sabatier says of revelation, "Being continuous,
the inspiration becomes normal, the ancient conflict between the divine
and the human vanishes . . . God lives and works in man, man lives and
works in God. Religion and nature, the voice divine and the voice of
conscience, the subject and the object of revelation, penetrate each other
and become one. The supreme revelation of God shines forth in the highest
of all consciousnesses and the loveliest of all human lives." *Ibid.*, p. 42. And
so with regard to authority in religion: "Then you no longer admit the
infallibility of the Bible. Why are you then scandalized when I perceive
and describe the inevitable and unconditional death of this old dogma? . . . It
is no longer the book which supports the truth of its teaching; it is the
elevation, the power, the general truth of the teaching, recognized by
the conscience, which supports the moral and religious authority of the
book . . . The outward authority of the letter has given place to the inward and purely moral authority of the Spirit." A. Sabatier, *The Religions
of Authority and the Religion of the Spirit* (New York: Williams and
Norgate, 1904), p. 259.

otherworldly invasion of God into that of a perfected social order, to be attained at the end of man's progressive development.[19] The loyal Christian did not wait in holiness and faith for salvation at the Last Day, but worked now within the world for peace, brotherhood, and human betterment. In contrast to both sectarianism and evangelicalism, liberalism interpreted the heart of its gospel, both as a theology and as an ethic, in cultural terms.[20]

This did not mean, however, that liberal religion enjoyed no inheritance from its sectarian origins. From them, at least in part, it took its antihierarchical, antisacramental, and anticreedal convictions. Again the church was given no dogmatic authority, nor did the minister represent or mediate such an authority. There were no holy liturgical symbols or sacraments, religion being purely personal and moral in character;[21] and the church was clearly under predominantly lay control. However, where the sectarian Christian, in repudiating the authority of priest and dogma, held himself under the absolute authority of a supernaturally revealed biblical word and law, the liberal knew no such transcendent and infallible divine authority over his life. On the contrary, his understanding of Christian truth was mediated

[19] The greatest interpreter of the liberal social gospel, Walter Rauschenbusch, redefined the Kingdom of God in these terms: "The Kingdom of God is humanity organized according to the will of God . . . Since Christ revealed the divine worth of life and personality, and since his salvation seeks the restoration and fulfillment of even the least, it follows that the Kingdom of God, at every stage of human development, tends towards a social order which will best guarantee to all personalities their freest and highest development." Again, "It is the Christian transfiguration of the social order." *A Theology for the Social Gospel* (New York: The MacMillan Co., 1918), pp. 142, 145.

[20] A vivid example of liberalism's interpretation of all aspects of religion in cultural, social terms is this recommendation of C. C. Morrison with regard to worship: "We must construct new models, new pageantry, new hymns, new forms of prayer, new anthems of praise, new dramatizations in which, for example, the labor movement may be caught up in the embrace of religion, the peace movement, the civic conscience, and the community spirit and the family, and every great human aspiration of our time." *The Social Gospel and the Christian Cultus* (New York: Harper & Brothers, 1933), pp. 67-68.

[21] On the whole, liberalism understood religion in two terms only: (1) with Schleiermacher, as personal and later individual religious experience or feelings, and (2) with Ritschl, as related solely to morality or spiritual freedom from the instinctive life. In neither case are the liturgical or sacra-

through the relativizing concepts and norms of culture, and his conceptions of Christian obligation were derived from and tested by the humanitarian and social ideals of democratic life.

For these reasons, from the viewpoint of conservative Protestantism, whether sectarian or evangelical, liberalism represented a complete capitulation to culture. Biblical categories were more often than not transformed into philosophical categories of development and progress derived from culture; and biblical law became liberal citizenship. There is some truth in this reproach, especially when one looks at that unique product of liberal culture-centered religion: the community church. Though they may not call themselves by this name, many urban churches are nowadays filled with folk from every denomination, and their way of life reflects no particular tradition or denominational history. The ethos of these churches is, therefore, nondenominational, noncreedal, nonsacramental, nonliturgical. If, then, shorn of tradition, they have also rejected the Bible as an absolute authority over their life, they can represent merely the spiritual and moral life of their social environment, expressing in their own life whatever that spiritual content may be. The goals of such churches are almost entirely the products of the hopes and aims of the surrounding community: community services of various sorts, psychological help, good politics in government, recreational programs, and so on. All these of course are very good, but they reflect no transcendent source, norm, or goal. There may well be a real element of transcendence, of the holy, in the life of many of these churches, but many also merely mediate to their community a message and a faith which that community has itself generated. Let us note how, with the community church, one final church-

---

mental elements of religious worship meaningful or relevant, involving as they do both communal and nonmoral factors. As an example of this, see the following from Kant, who set much of the tone of at least the second, or moral, form of liberalism: "Whatever, over and above good life conduct, man fancies that he can do to become well-pleasing to God is mere religious illusion and pseudo-service of God." Immanuel Kant, *Religion Within the Limits of Pure Reason* (New York: Harper Torchbook, 1960), p. 158. Small wonder that the postliberal generation has had difficulties with worship! In the same vein, the writer's father has often related how, decades ago, a well-known scholar and president of Union Theological Seminary used to come into church on Sunday regularly at 11:30 A.M., so as to hear the sermon but miss the service of worship that preceded.

type element has stolen back into free church life: the parish idea, one church as inclusive of the entire community—say, a new suburban development—blessing and helping it, but not radically transforming or separating itself from it. And let us also note how the church-type practice of infant baptism creeps forward as Baptists and Disciples baptize their infants at twelve, eleven, or even nine years old, so that they will "grow up in the church home," and so as to "get them in the church before high school turns them away from Christianity"—both completely church-type sentiments.

On the other side of the ledger, it must be said that of the two responses liberal Christianity has been immeasurably the more creative. Although it has tended often to lose sight of the transcendent element in the church, it has more than justified its existence by insisting on the relevance of Christian faith to all man's secular life. First, liberal theology made it possible for a man to live creatively in the scientific thought world of modern culture without losing touch with his own faith. Since he was living in the culture anyway and making use of the technology produced by science, this honesty has been spiritually important. But still more significant, liberal Christianity insisted, for almost the first time in Christian history, that the ethical standards of the gospel were relevant to the structures of man's social life. It was liberalism that saw that the forms of society which produced injustice, oppression, exploitation, or suffering are as antithetical to Christian faith as the varied forms of personal vice. Liberalism understood rightly, in other words, that social structures and problems are as intimately related to sin and redemption as are personal habits of drink or lust.[22] Thus the sectarian insight that a Christian life is a total communal existence obedient to the Christian gospel has, in the liberal social gospel, moved creatively *into* society and has now applied the same affir-

[22] With regard to sin in its social forms, Rauschenbusch had the following to say: "To find the climax of sin we must not linger over a man who swears, or sneers at religion, or denies the mystery of the Trinity, but put our hands on social groups who have turned the patrimony of a nation into the private property of a small class, or have left the peasant laborers cowed, degraded, demoralized, and without rights in the land. When we find such in history, or in present-day life, we shall know we have struck real rebellion against God on the higher levels of sin." *Op. cit.,* p. 50.

mation of communal relevance to the whole social order. If Christian man is in fact a participant in culture, then his economic, political, and social activities as voter, businessman, and member of a particular class and race come under Christian norms and judgement as clearly as do his individual habits. This is true, and the only possible understanding of Christian obligation for man in culture. And this emphasis on the relevance of the gospel to all our daily life is the most precious heritage we have received from liberalism.

Interestingly enough, this insistence on the relevance of the gospel to man's social existence produced the one real element of transcendence in recent American denominational life. Although it was often expressed in seemingly secular terms—for example, in semisocialist categories or in the categories of progress—the liberal social gospel has been the one vital point where the church has challenged its own culture with radical intensity. Liberal religion seldom used the phrases of sin and judgment, but in liberal churches, North and South alike, where the economic, political, racial, and international sins of the congregation and community have been condemned, there was and is more sense of divine judgment and correspondingly of real contrition for actual sins than in conservative churches, where the old words are used but the relevant sins—such as those of race and of unreasoning nationalism—are never mentioned.

In this example we find one real clue to the discovery of the holy and the transcendent. The holy and transcendent is that which is ultimately relevant to our existence, both as a whole and in all its various facets. While finding no origin in our immediate social and natural environment, the holy is nevertheless that which alone is relevant to every relation the self can have to its whole world, for it is the basis of our relation to these environments, and it is the source and ground of *their* being and meaning as well as of our own. The holy, therefore, can never be completely separated from the secular world it is meant to undergird without thereby losing its holiness, as the history of the church amply demonstrates. For with separation it ceases to be that which undergirds, conditions, and directs all that we do. As the example of conservative Protestantism has shown, wherever doctrine or religious experience become unrelated to the

world of secular thought and affairs, they too, then, become
merely special and finite portions of existence, "Sunday activities" and "preacher's talk"—and having lost their relevance to
our total life, lose thereby the depth and universality that bespeak
true holiness. The separated world of religion is in this sense no
longer "holy," for its Lord is closeted in too small a realm. Perhaps the realm is that of special sacraments and rites, or, as here,
of limited personal purity, special inward experience, and the
final fate of our individual souls. In either case transcendence and
true holiness are lost to such an esoteric, private deity. Correspondingly, if religion becomes merely the world, it, too, becomes too parochial, private, and special, but in a different sense,
reflecting now only the customs and conventions of a special
society. The religious or holy, then, is properly not a category
either totally separated from the secular or completely identified
with it. Rather it is that which relates us to the source of our
life and the goal of its meaning, and thus that which conditions
and ultimately directs all our secular existence.[23] When the transcendent in religion ceases to have immediate relevance for our
secular thought and behavior, the transcendence itself dissolves,
and the religion in question becomes a merely social affair,
separated from all importance and devoid of divine authority or
transforming power. Wherever, therefore, there is social or religious complacency, wherever congregations are "at home in

[23] For this reason, while assenting to much of their analysis of our current
situation, one cannot subscribe to the sharp either/or between "religion"
and "secularity" characteristic of Bonhoeffer and those whom he has influenced. Here, apparently, a man must choose between participation in the
thought and life of the secular world on the one hand and in religion on
the other. If he wishes to be part of the world of affairs and of modern
thought, he must relinquish the religious; if he retains his concern with the
latter, then he must, it seems, abdicate from the life and the thinking of
the world. For example: "Either 'being a Christian' is something 'religious'
and quite distinct from secular affairs, or Christian faith is a human posture
conceivable for a man who is part of his secular culture." Paul Van Buren,
The Secular Meaning of the Gospel (New York, The Macmillan Co., 1963),
p. 17. If the "religious" is thus inevitably separate from and so irrelevant
to the secular world in which we all live, then for us it has thereby ceased
to participate in the holy and the transcendent, and has become merely a
part—an irrelevant part—of the culture in which it lives but which it now
ignores. Many necessary and unpleasant choices do face us, but this choice
between abandoning all religious categories of thought and life or abandoning the world around us, is not, I feel, one of them—though the radical

Zion,"[24] there—whatever the *formally* orthodox or holy character of their theology—the transcendent has vanished and with it any vestige of the holy.

Liberalism tended to lose the transcendent in favor of culture in the areas of belief, authority, and worship; but its ethical passion for making the gospel relevant preserved in it a vital mediation of the Word of God to our time. Wherever that ethical passion was lost, however, the dependence of liberalism on secular culture for its beliefs and ethical standards, and its humanistic patterns of worship, meant that it too was intensely vulnerable to culture. When one visits present-day community churches, one often cannot decide whether the wisdom of Freud or the goals of the men's luncheon clubs are more dominant in their life.

Neither resolution, therefore, is ultimately satisfactory. Conservative Protestantism maintains its transcendence only in the forms of a fading dogma and a biblical literalism irrelevant to man's concrete life. Thus where important decisions are actually made, conservative Protestantism has in most cases capitulated to culture. And liberalism, in turn, has in itself no structural elements that can mediate transcendence and judgment. Whenever its social passion is lost or dissipated, it too capitulates to culture.

In both these forms of "culture religion" we see implicit the danger that faces American Christianity in our present world conflict. For it is very possible that the democratic, capitalistic culture with which in America these two forms have amalgamated will soon find itself in mortal conflict with a Communist culture whose "natural laws" and concepts of the good society are diametrically opposed to the American view. In such a case the culturation of these two forms of religion can become demonic, in so far as either one ceases to be able to judge its own cultural base and becomes merely a mode of condemning

---

rethinking of our theology in the light of the world's thought is, one must agree, a choice we cannot dodge. Perhaps one could say that the present secularity of the world puts almost irresistible psychological pressure on us to reject religious categories, but that it puts similar logical pressure on us has not been demonstrated—and I often feel that both the Bultmannians and the Bonhoefferans have tended to confuse these two kinds of pressure.

[24] Amos 6:1.

the national enemy. The relative power of transcendence in each of these forms of denominational religion may well be tested by Communism in the next few years: whether a supernatural gospel that ignores culture and yet lives in and from it, or a humanistic faith that seeks to enshrine the best in culture, can generate the most transcendence over the culture itself. On present evidence, my money is on the liberal tradition. But at the same time one must admit that social gospel pulpits are rare, and where that gospel is absent there is little contest and therefore little to choose between the two.

In the next three chapters, by discussing three central biblical symbols of the church, I shall attempt to show how the church can deal creatively with this situation, so that the perils of conformity to culture may be changed into opportunities for its transformation.

3

The People of God

Our analysis up to this point has indicated that the secret of the church's relation to the world in which it lives is a dialectic or tension between transcendence and relevance. The church, we believe, is established by God's act and nourished by His Word. It lives, therefore, from divine authority and divine grace: that is its sole importance and the sole justification for its existence at all. Without this it becomes merely a cultural piety of little use to anyone. But as we have found, this relation to the divine is maintained only if the transcendent, noncultural, separated elements in the church's life have an immediate relevance to the total life of man. Only if they are related continuously and creatively to every facet of his daily existence in the world can they retain their transcendence. If, then, man is *in* culture—if he is "secular man"—these transcendent elements must be in continual tension and relation to his life and culture, to his scientific and philosophical ideas, his social habits, and his community mores.

As we saw in the last chapter, both answers of American Protestantism have a hold on partial aspects of this truth, and both have lost sight of other aspects. Conservative Protestantism has emphasized the preservation of the transcendent, authoritative elements: against all cultural influences it has insisted on the sanctity of biblical doctrine and fundamentals, and the necessity of a special experience of divine grace for salvation. But because it has failed to keep that doctrine related to cultural ideas, its transcendent authority has been sacrificed. It floats above the life of the church affirmed by everyone but irrelevant to daily life. And because, having moved into culture, conservative Protestantism failed to mediate the judgment of God on the culture it embraced, its original sense of the transcendence and holiness of the divine has been vanishing from the life of its respectable congregations. Without relevance, the transcendence of the transcendent is soon lost, and the church is acclimatized to culture. Liberal Protestantism, on the other hand, emphasized the relevance of the gospel to all of life and thus achieved a unique measure of transcendence of the church over against the evil structures of human society. But although it freed man from the tyranny of old dogmatisms and ecclesiastical authority, nevertheless it provided no lasting defenses against the tyranny of culture. If it also becomes too acclimatized to American culture and merely repeats in pious language the thoughts and goals of our national life, then in relinquishing its transcendence it, too, will lose its relevance—so are relevance and transcendence inextricably intermixed in religion.

The problem, as we have noted, has been in large part created by the social changes in American church life. The sects have moved into culture, losing thereby those elements of biblical absoluteness, emotional experience, and communal ethic which were maintained by their separateness from secular influence. Correspondingly, there has not yet evolved any viable form of church life *within* culture which can maintain both the divine authority, on the one hand, and the sectarian values of personal freedom and relevance to our everyday, secular lives, on the other. This is the major task of the church in our generation if Protestantism is to remain creative.

One could put this problem in terms of a series of questions:

1. How is the church to mediate the divine authority to men

in word, worship, and behavior so that this authority is not merely dogmatic, sterile, and irrelevant—a separate, protected, but useless realm of the "religious," unrelated to the world?

2. How is it to affirm the freedom of its members as cultural beings to live within society, to think as they see fit, and to govern their lives as their own consciences guide them—how is it to affirm its joyful acceptance of the world—without losing completely the transcendent, holy elements within itself?

3. How can the church in its message be concerned with culture, relevant to cultural problems and issues, and intelligible to people who live in culture, without surrendering to the domination of the various "religions" of culture with their dubious standards and goals?

4. How can the church in its government be ruled with the full participation of the congregation, as we believe it should be, without surrendering its sovereignty and standards to Main Street?

These are, I believe, the most fundamental questions that face Protestantism in America today. In order to answer them in this new situation, the mere repetition of our old official language of the church, the ministry, worship, and Christian behavior is not enough. What is needed is a radical rethinking of our understanding of these things.

It has been traditional in Protestantism that when such basic theological questions are raised about our dilemmas and God's resolution of them, we go to the Scriptures for guidance in formulating our answers. And thus it is, too, with the church—for what we are asking here is how the church can, in our situation, be itself and perform its task; surely it is our common assumption as a Christian community that only from a biblical understanding of the church can we receive the answer.

Our problem was, as we uncovered it, that the church's task involved the mediation of the transcendent, of the holy, to man's cultural existence, and that the denomination, as it now appears, seems unable to offer this. The traditional holy elements of the church-type churches it rejects, and in embracing cultural life it has been forced to relinquish its own sectarian means of preserving the holy. What we are searching for, then, are valid and pertinent ways in which to rethink the denominational

church in the light of its new social situation, so that it can become a vehicle of the holy to today's world. And this can only
be done by uncovering the primary biblical symbols of the transcendent in the church's life, and asking how they are relevant
to the present historical situation of the church as our analysis
has revealed it.

Three central biblical symbols of the church have, in its long
history, been overwhelmingly significant for it, determining its
understanding of itself and so guiding its self-formation. Through
them, therefore, and the way each of them impinges on the life
of the contemporary church, we may be helped to recover our
relation to the transcendent and thus to mediate the holy to the
world. For each points to one aspect of holiness in the original
and essential form of the church, and so—appropriately enough
—each has been the dominant symbol for one of the various
interpretations of the church that history has in fact produced.
These symbols are (a) the church as the People of God, the
New Israel, or the new humanity—the symbol dear to our sectarian forefathers; (b) Jesus Christ as the Lord of the church
through His holy Word—the symbol central to the Reformation;
and (c) the church as the Body of Christ—the symbol around
which Catholicism has centered its thought. Let us begin then
with the first of these: the church as the People of God.

The free-church tradition has rightly held that the church in
the New Testament is primarily a congregation, a fellowship of
people; neither a building nor a clerical heirarchy but a community.[1] And this is emphasized by the word used for it: "ec-

---

[1] Especially in his earlier writings (before 1525) Luther had of course
likewise insisted that the church is primarily a congregation or fellowship,
a *Gemeinde* (*Gemeine* in archaic German) rather than a hierarchy.
He uses the word *Gemeinde* in defining the church as "the congregation, or assembly of the saints, i.e., the pious, believing men on earth,
which is gathered, preserved, and ruled by the Holy Ghost." "A Brief
Explanation of . . . the Creed," Third Part, *Works of Martin Luther*, Vol.
II (Philadelphia: Muhlenberg Press, 1943), p. 373. See also the same definition in "The Papacy at Rome," *ibid.*, Vol. I, p. 349. And his continual
reiteration of the priesthood of believers and so of the equality of all
Christians underlines the same point (cf. "An Open Letter to the
Christian Nobility," *ibid.*, Vol. II, p. 69; also "Concerning the Ministry,"
Luther's Works, J. Pelikan, ed., Vol. 40 (St. Louis, Mo.: Concordia, 1958),
pp. 9, 19, 37.) However, two qualifications should be made of his "con-

clesia," a gathering of people called out by God into a new kind
of community.[2] But we must go on to ask: What kind of a community, what kind of a people, is this ecclesia? In answer to this
question, in the New Testament we continually come across the
symbols or ideas just mentioned. For the earliest church understood itself as a people in two ways: first, as the New Israel—
that is, as the continuation and renewal of the convenant community, the chosen people of God, the Jews; and secondly, as
embodying a new humanity, the renewal of a total creation that
had fallen in Adam but had now risen to new life in Jesus Christ.

The first thing, therefore, that an early Christian would have
said if we had asked him, "What is your congregation, your new
fellowship?" would have been, "We are the people who are the
heirs of the promises to Abraham, we are the people of the new
covenant, we are the true Israel."[3] Now, this symbol of the New
Israel is of the greatest significance for our understanding of the
church. It means, first of all, that the church is not an accidental,
secondary element in the Christian faith—as if God had really
willed to save individuals, who through misguided gregarious
instinct and evil power-impulses mistakenly formed for themselves a community of worship. Rather, the symbol makes clear
that the church as a community of believers is a fundamental
part of the divine purpose, willed by God and established by

gregational" view of the church: (1) the meaning of "congregation" here
is not that of a specific local community of people actually related to each
other, so much as that of *all* believing Christians everywhere, who therefore do not form an actual community. (Calvin has the same meaning
when he defines the church as "the whole multitude dispersed over all the
world." John Calvin, *Institutes of the Christian Religion*, trans. by J. Allen
[Philadelphia: Presbyterian Board of Christian Education, 1936], Bk. III,
Chap. I, sec. 7.) (2) After 1525 Luther put less emphasis on the congregation as the seat of validity and authority in the church and more on the
church as bearer of the sacred Word—see Ernst Troeltsch, *The Social
Teachings of the Christian Churches* (New York: The Macmillan Co.,
1949), Vol. II, pp. 515-44. Thus it is fair to say that the real bearers of the
notion that the church centers in the local congregation as the actual community of believers are the sectarian writers, as evidenced by the notes
concerning them in Chap. II above.

[2] Cf. K. L. Schmidt, *The Church*, from Gerhard Kittel's *Theologisches
Wörterbuch* (London: Adam and Charles Black, 1950), pp. 1, 10, 14-15, and
especially 24.

[3] Acts 13:16-34; Rom. 4:12-17, 22-25; Gal. 3:29, 4:28-29; Eph. 3:5-6; Heb.
8:4-13, 9, 10; I Pet. 1:10-12, 2:1-10.

him just as much as the Incarnation itself. For the covenant
people Israel was a creation of God, and thus the church as the
continuation of Israel is also God's creation. The church, therefore, is a vital part of the gospel itself, one of the great gifts we
have been given by God throughout the whole history of his
dealings with men.

For what we find in the Old Testament is the story of the
creation of a unique community through a series of divine
covenantal acts and revelations.[4] The Jews had no sense that
they of themselves had created the people Israel—that the divine
covenant had, so to speak, been made first with individual Jews
who then covenanted themselves into a community, as many
free-church thinkers seem to believe. Rather, the religious consciousness that runs through the whole Old Testament is that
God called this community into being, and only by being a full
member of God's community through obedience to God's law
could a Jew inherit its blessings. It was God who had called
Abraham and made it possible for him to become the father of
the people; it was God who had summoned Moses to his mighty
task, had rescued the people and forged them into a religious
community through the law at Sinai. And it was God who had
over and over again called the community back to its true nature
through the prophets. The whole great sweep of the Old Testament is the enthralling story of the creation by God Himself
of a "holy people," a kingdom of priests, a new kind of human
community.

Throughout their history there is one theme that grows in
strength as the story develops. It is that they can become God's
people only if in their community life they are obedient to the
divine law enshrined in the covenant. More and more the external ceremonies and rites of their earlier religious life recede
in significance, and the call to moral obedience comes forward.
"What does the Lord require of thee, but to do justly, and to
love mercy, and to walk humbly with thy God?"[5] The character

[4] Exod. 19:4-6, 29:45-6; Isa. 43:1-7, 49:1-12; Amos 3:1-2; Mic. 6:4. See also
Walter Eichrodt, *Theology of the Old Testament*, trans. by J. A. Baker
(Philadelphia: Westminster Press, 1961), Vol. I, Chaps. II and III; G. E.
Wright, *The Book of the Acts of God* (Garden City, N.Y.: Doubleday &
Co., 1957), Chap. I; B. W. Anderson, *Understanding the Old Testament*
(Englewood, N.J.: Prentice-Hall, 1957), Introduction.

of the people whom God is fashioning is, according to the prophets, one structured along lines of justice and mercy, a community in which the poor are neither robbed nor oppressed, and the widow and the fatherless are cared for and protected. The love (agape) that is to be characteristic of the Christian community is not yet explicitly described, but the prophetic understanding of what God's law required was moving rapidly in that direction. God's purpose, then, in forming this people was to create a new kind of people morally, among whom mercy replaces vindictiveness, justice oppression, and every man has his respected place. As the prophets realized, only a remnant is thus obedient to the divine law, and in Christian eyes there is at the end only one man—our Lord Himself—who lives thus righteously and with love. But this sad history of betrayal does not negate the divine purpose that men shall live as God's people in harmony with one another. Thus when the early church calls itself the New Israel, it is saying a great deal about the character of its communal existence: that it is the continuation of the long history in which God has been creating this holy people, now reconstituted through the life, death, and resurrection of Christ. And secondly, that through the power of Christ the church takes for itself the calling of becoming the holy People of God who fulfill the divine will of justice and love one to another.

The church, however, is not only a continuation of the original covenant People of God. A second symbol is put along side that of the New Israel. The church also understands itself as a new beginning on even wider terms: a new beginning for the whole human race. For its center is not now the divine law addressed to a *particular* people; rather it is the crucified and risen Lord

⁵ Mic. 6:8. Cf. also: "To what purpose is the multitude of your sacrifices unto me? saith the Lord: I am full of the burnt offerings of rams, and the fat of fed beasts . . . Bring no more vain oblations; incense is an abomination to me . . . Wash you, make you clean; put away the evil of your doings from before mine eyes; cease to do evil; learn to do well; seek judgment, relieve the oppressed, judge the fatherless, plead for the widow" (Isa. 1:10-17). "I hate, I despise your feast days, and I take no delight in your solemn assemblies. Even though you offer me your burnt offerings and cereal offerings, I will not accept them . . . But let justice run down like waters, and righteousness like an everflowing stream" (Amos 5:21-24). Cf. also Isa. 5:8-23; Hos. 4:1-2; Amos 2:4-8, 4:1-2, 8:4-10; and Mic. 2:1-2, 3:1-4, 7:1-7.

who has come that all men might be brought into the People of God. The church is, in other words, the new humanity in Christ.[6] "As in Adam all die, so in Christ are all made alive," said Paul, affirming thereby that in Christ—that is, in the new covenant people—the whole community of mankind is to be refashioned by the divine purpose and gracious will. Thus in its reconstitution in Christ the holy People of God has been widened and its life deepened immeasurably. In place of justice and law there is now the work of the Holy Spirit which is love, effecting the closest sort of personal unity among the members; in fact, for the earliest church the crowning test of discipleship, and so of membership in the community, was the love of each for the

[6] Rom. 3:23-31, and esp. 5:12-21; I Cor. 1:22-24. This theme of the new humanity, a new race, a new beginning for mankind as a whole, continues in the early church. "You would also like to know the source of the loving affection that they have for each other. You wonder, too, why this new race or way of life has appeared on earth now and not earlier." "The So-called Letter to Diognetus" (c. 123-124 or 129), Sec. 1, *Early Christian Fathers*, trans. and ed. by C. C. Richardson, Library of Early Christian Classics, Vol. I (Philadelphia: Westminster Press, 1953), p. 213. And this same theme of a new or recapitulated race of men was given classic expression by Irenaeus in the late second century: ". . . so did He who is the Word, recapitulating Adam in himself, rightly receive a birth, enabling Him to gather up Adam [into Himself], from Mary . . . If, then, the first Adam had a man for his father, and was born of human seed, it were reasonable to say that the Second Adam was begotten of Joseph. But if the former was taken from the dust, and God was his maker, it was incumbent that the latter also, making a recapitulation in Himself, should be formed as man by God . . ." Irenaeus, *Against Heresies*, Bk. III, Chap. XXI, sec. 10, found in *The Ante-Nicene Fathers*, Vol. I (Grand Rapids, Mich.: Eerdmans, 1950), p. 454. "It was necessary, therefore, that the Lord, coming to the lost sheep, and making recapitulation of so comprehensive a dispensation, and seeking after His own handiwork, should save that very man who had been created after His image and likeness, that is, Adam . . . [This was necessary,] too, inasmuch as the whole economy of salvation regarding man came to pass according to the good pleasure of the Father, in order that God might not be conquered . . . For if man, who had been created by God that he might live, after losing life . . . should not any more return to life, but should be utterly [and for ever] abandoned to death, God would [in that case] have been conquered . . ." *Ibid.*, Chap. XXIII, sec. 1, p. 455. Thus was the new community of Christians regarded as a new beginning of the entire race of men, brought out of sin and death into love and eternal life by Jesus Christ.

It is the symbol of the new humanity which, more than any other in ecclesiology, provides the basis for the mission of the church. For in this understanding, Christ has come for the salvation of all men, of all races, nations, and classes, and therefore the church is called upon to proclaim its

other.[7] And all barriers between men are broken down by the spirit of love within this new humanity in Christ: "There is neither Jew nor Greek, bond nor free, male nor female, for ye are all one in Christ Jesus."[8]

What an amazing picture of the church is presented to us through this apostolic symbol of the People of God: the recreation of human community around Christ into a community of love! In Adam all men had died; in our sinful history, in other words, the created differences between men, differences of sex, race, culture, and nationality have become, not a source of richness within a common human community, but the source of mistrust, exploitation, conflict, hatred, and tragedy. Some have

---

gospel and to open its doors to every living human creature. Since the people of God who listen for his Word, who obey his commandments, and who seek His presence in worship are in principle the whole of humanity, this task of mission can never cease—and any church that has lost this consciousness of seeking the lost beyond its own boundaries, as well as the lost within them, has to that extent ceased to be faithful to its given task.

This writer is, however, hesitant to define the church in terms of its mission, as some have done—to locate the central "mark" of the church there. Mission is a necessary activity of the church, but it does not and cannot constitute its essence. There are two reasons for this. First, if people all concentrate solely or even mainly on making other people Christians, they are apt to cease being concerned about being Christian themselves; they come to take this for granted and thus tend to forget the means of grace by which they and any they may convert are enabled to be in relation to God. As a consequence and secondly, if the church is concerned solely with expanding its membership, with bringing people in, then there is nothing substantial there to offer the new convert—or the old missioner—when he is finally persuaded to join. Some groups, notably in our day the Southern Baptists, have made evangelism the central core of the church, and their experience reveals the problem involved. For then ministers tend to be taught, not how to care for their flock by preaching, counseling, and worship, but how to evangelize—i.e., how to persuade other people to join the flock. And when these new members ask, "Now that I have joined, what am I to do?" the answer is apt to be "Go out among your neighbors and bring in some more"—who, presumably, will in turn themselves merely seek new additions among their neighbors. Being a Christian thus becomes merely the activity of making more Christians, and being a church becomes merely the operation of expanding itself. And with this the religious reality of Christianity, both as a personal relation to God through the hearing of His Word and the worship of His glory, and the incarnating of that Word in acts of love and reconciliation, is in danger of being lost. Important as is the passing on of the faith to others, nevertheless that faith itself, and so the community that holds it, must consist of more than the process of passing it on. A relay team whose members themselves never actually ran, but only

become enslaved, some oppressed, most excluded from being neighbors one to another. Barriers of religion, race, class, and nation have arisen out of sin and destroyed community among men, who were created for love. But now in Christ a new age has arrived. The old humanity of sin is to be cast off, and men have in Christ become new creatures who are to serve rather than to oppress one another, and love rather than hate. In the church these amazing powers of the Kingdom are, moreover, manifested. In its life this final purpose of God for a new humanity has, through Christ, at last become a reality. For in the church is the Spirit which is the bond of peace and love among men. As barriers and hatred and conflict characterized the old human community, so koinonia—forbearance in love and unity in the Spirit—is the animating life of this community. In this deepest sense the church has become the holy People of God—so says our symbol, pointing as it does to the ethical purpose of the church as a community of men—that is, to the divine law for its social existence.

---

handed on the baton to other "runners," would win no races; so a church that seeks only to add to its own rolls has hardly any time to be the church.

7 Cf. I John 1:7-11, 3:10-11, 4:7-8, 12-13. And let us note Augustine's commentary on this text: "Love is the only final distinction between the sons of God and the sons of the devil. All may sign themselves with the sign of Christ's cross: all may answer Amen . . . all may be baptized, all may come to Church and line the walls of our places of meeting. But there is nothing to distinguish the sons of God from the sons of the devil save charity. They that have charity, are born of God: they that have not charity are not . . ." "Fifth Homily on I John," sec. 7, found in *Augustine's Later Works*, John Burnaby, ed., Library of Christian Classics, Vol. VIII (Philadelphia: Westminster Press, 1955), p. 298. "Your brother is hungry, in want: maybe he is in trouble, hard pressed by some creditor. He has not what he needs, you have. He is your brother, he and you were purchased together, one price was paid for both of you, both were redeemed by the blood of Christ . . . Do you ask, what concern is it of mine? Am I to give my money to save him from inconvenience? If that is the answer your heart gives you, the love of the Father dwells not in you; and if the love of the Father dwells not in you, you are not born of God. How can you boast of being a Christian? You have the name and not the deeds." *Ibid.,* sec. 12, pp. 301-302.

8 Gal. 3:28; Col. 3:11; I Cor. 12:13; also Rom. 12:4. Again let us listen to Augustine on the relation of love to equality: "The true Christian will never set himself up over other men . . . If you would be better than another man, you will grudge to see him as your equal. You ought to wish all men equal to yourself; and if you have gone beyond another man in wisdom, you should want him too to show himself wise . . . See how he [Paul] wanted

When we look at this awesome meaning of the church in the New Testament, we can only feel very repentant for our own life. We free churchmen often pride ourselves that we have "restored" the primitive Christian church of the first century. What we actually mean is that we have abstracted for our concentration only the most external aspects of that church. All too often we have left out the more important and much more difficult meaning of "congregation" or "ecclesia": the new community of God held together by love, and so free of all the old barriers of sin. And those free-church traditions which have emphasized so strongly the standards of personal commitment and personal holiness if the church is to be the church, are here especially in need of repentance: by these very standards of what makes a true church, namely, obedience by the total membership, have we really been the holy People of God as the New Testament portrays that people?

Let us look at our actual situation. How does our denominational church, situated in suburbia and characterized by its white middle-class clientele, compare with this weighted symbol, with this moral law that is to characterize the church's life? Obviously our churches have not fulfilled this law of their being, for they have by no means conquered the barriers of the world but merely reproduced them again in their own congregations. Instead of the community of Christ being a new humanity of love, it has become "conformed to this world" and has recreated the barriers of Jew and Greek, slave and free, black and white, in its own midst. It is with some relief that we realize that this betrayal has always been true in some part. According to Robert Brown, there appears in a late medieval manuscript this astounding sentence: "The Church is something like Noah's ark; if it weren't for the storm outside, we could not stand the smell inside."[9] We should not, however, let the ubiquity of this problem blind us to the truth that our own life is in fact a denial of the meaning of the symbol.

---

all to be his equals; and just because charity made him so desire, he was raised above all. Man has transgressed his proper limit . . . he has let covetousness carry him away, so that he might be higher than other men, and that is pride." "Eighth Homily on I John," sec. 8, *op. cit.*, pp. 321-22.

[9] Robert McAfee Brown, *The Significance of the Church* (Philadelphia: Westminster Press, 1956), p. 17. Although Prof. Brown does not credit this

The history of the free churches with regard to this matter of fellowship is interesting and, as usual, ironic. We have seen that the original sectarian groups gathered themselves out of the barrier-ridden world. Condemning the privileges of the world as sinful, they formed communities where there were no lords or peasants, owners or slaves, rulers or ruled, but only simple Christians. Thus, as the Anabaptist peasants sang, "equality and justice among men are basic gifts of the Holy Spirit,"[10] and Quakers, in the way they dressed, acted, and spoke to all men, refused to recognize any differences of rank. In such groups, which all could join whatever their former rank in the world, the words "Christian fellowship" had definite meaning, namely a bond of relationship that transcended the artificial barriers of society. The sense of comradeship, of real koinonia, that was generated in these separated fellowships of equals, especially under persecution, gave an entirely different meaning to the church, one that had not been known since its earliest history. In Catholicism the church was a divine and mysterious institution resident in its clerical hierarchy and massive edifices, related to and participated in by each person as a lone individual through the priest and through the sacraments. Here people from all ranks entered the church, to be sure, but they paid no attention to one another, nor did they have any human "communion" with each other, each taking part in sermon and sacrament in accordance with his own rank in society. Suddenly in the sects the church became a *Gemeinde*, a fellowship of people, a congregation. To be in the church meant, therefore, actually to participate in a closely bound community of people which knew no limits, since all could enter through confession of faith, but whose bonds were of infinite closeness because it was a community of mutual help and sharing, mutual judgment and forgiveness.

Brought to this country by the free churches, this communal understanding of the church as a people received, of course, vast encouragement from the egalitarian character of American

---

saying to the saint known as Hereticus, general stylistic features might lead one's mind in that direction.

[10] Cf. Art. III of the "Twelve Articles" of the peasants in Schwabia, *Works of Martin Luther*, Vol. IV (Philadelphia: Muhlenberg Press, 1931), p. 213.

life and from the obvious value of such fellowship in the American wilderness. Thus the concept of the church as a closely knit community of people is taken for granted in American denominational life and is the most characteristic thing that foreigners notice about our churches. A Lutheran church in Germany is like a theater; you go alone, listen to the Word, and leave alone, ungreeted by older members—who very likely do not even know each other—and surely uninvited to conversation or to dinner. By contrast, in every church in America, once outside the East, a visitor finds himself besieged by welcomers, official and unofficial, pulled into the coffee hour, and often invited home to a Sunday meal. The subsequent power of this tradition in American life can be seen in the fact that even in our Episcopal and Catholic churches the same greeting committees and friendly coffee hours prevail as in the Baptist and Methodist. The church here is a closely bound fellowship, where ideally everyone is friendly with everyone else, where church relations and social relations have been remarkably synonymous—where people regularly eat together, entertain each other, and marry one another.

But this story of congregational fellowship has a sting in its tail. For as these groups have moved up into middle-class society, the friendliness has subtly changed character and scope. Earlier, as we noted, it included all ranks of society indifferently, for the fellowship was itself apart from social rank. Thus bond and free, duke and peasant, could freely enter sectarian groups and be welcome. Now, however, the fellowship is that of middle-class white people, and while it retains all its old warmth, it has vastly restricted its limits. How can these gentle suburban folk be expected to be friendly with a truck-driver or a Negro? Could they consider having fellowship with such a one, eating with him and entertaining him in their homes? As one said to me, "church is where you meet your kind of people, and therefore where you can make friends and associate with them."[11]

[11] This remark reflects one of the central theses of Gibson Winter's book, namely that the suburban locus of the churches makes homogeneity the main principle of congregational association: "The new image of the Church is a reflection of the dominant principle of association in American life, economic integration: people in a metropolitan area associate with one another on the basis of similar occupations, prestige, income, residence, and

The very closeness of the fellowship in sectarian churches has made it doubly difficult for them, once they have achieved the upper reaches of society, to transcend the narrow limits that their class status forces upon them. On the other hand, the church-type churches, with few of the traditionally built-in requirements for close personal fellowship of suppers and mutual entertainment, and with a chain of definite authority that reaches beyond local prejudices, have been able to integrate the classes and races of our society within themselves far more quickly. The very groups which first dispensed with the ranks and privileges of the world in the name of a close koinonia have become—ironically, precisely because of their emphasis on fellowship—the worst examples in our society of conformity to the ranks and standards of the world. It is obvious that these various levels of society now take precedence, and so determine the people with whom churchmen will have "Christian fellowship," while in their history just the opposite was the case. Somehow our free churches, whose essential symbol has been that of the People of God, must reverse their more lately acquired priorities and let the character and demands of a truly Christian koinonia, which knows none of society's ranks, determine the membership of their community.

A vivid example will illustrate the ironical duality of the

---

style of life." *The Suburban Captivity of the Churches* (Garden City, N.Y.: Doubleday & Co., 1961), p. 62. "Since churches organize their congregations or parishes primarily around residential neighborhoods and secondarily around family ties, congregations can be expected to mirror the economic ladder which determines place of residence. Each congregation will tend to become a cluster of people of like social and economic position." *Ibid.*, p. 66. That this, however, is not a problem in Protestant congregations alone is evidenced by Father Fichter's study of a New Orleans Roman Catholic parish—though a Protestant should humbly add that they do much better than we. "It may be said that in this system of socially segregated parishes, according to which the territorial boundaries of white and Negro parishes overlap, there can be little expectation of social solidarity based on Christian love across racial lines. The social bond of the mystical body which is presumed to unite baptized persons regardless of race is empirically insignificant in comparison with the practical day-to-day effect of racial separation." J. H. Fichter, S.J., *Social Relations in the Urban Parish* (Chicago: University of Chicago Press, 1954), p. 48. And after a study of the interrelations of women in the parish, he concludes: "The general fact is that the large majority conform to the institutionalized class patterns and neglect the social virtues which are implied in the Christian religion." *Ibid.*, p. 119.

modern free church. I attended one Sunday service devoted to missionary outreach in a suburban Baptist church in Nashville, Tennessee, where a young Baptist missionary just back from Italy told of his successes abroad. In glowing terms he spoke of how "gospel Christianity" had in Italy "broken down all the barriers of that society. Why," said he, "in my little group in Milan there are an ex-Communist, a laborer, a former aristocrat, a merchant, and even an ex-Catholic"—all these former ranks and stations of that effete society having been transcended in the power of evangelical religion! And of course the congregation in Nashville was enraptured by this heart-warming message of how the unpretentious Southern Baptist gospel had so leveled all these unreasonable Italian barriers—barriers which they all knew were, as one dear elderly lady said, against God's will. In this enthusiasm for the social triumph of the Baptist gospel in Italy there was not the slightest consciousness that that same gospel had so far made absolutely no dent on the rigid racial and class barriers dominating the life of that happy church in suburban Nashville. This silly story shows how crucial the sociological locus of a congregation is to its ethical success—for the same American gospel in Italy or India may shatter social barriers it cannot budge on its home ground, where it has itself become entrenched in the structures of society. This also shows that the building of the Kingdom of God must begin where it is most difficult, with those divisions between people in which we ourselves participate and of which we are, therefore, almost totally unaware.

As I have tried to indicate throughout these three chapters, the present confusion with regard to the ethical requirements of modern church life is so great as almost to defy analysis. Hovering over all feelings on this subject is, of course, the older anti-vice ethic, agreed on by all as "what Christianity means for our life," but tacitly applied only to the minister's existence. What, in this new situation of a two-level ethic, Christianity means in the way of conduct and standards for the layman is quite unknown, as yet unconceived, and almost never preached on—the minister's ethic being apparently the sole subject of discussion. It may be noted that nothing would be so fruitful in the local church as to begin such a discussion among laymen, honestly recognizing the fact that the two-level ethic exists and makes irrelevant the older anti-vice definition of Christian virtue, and then seeking to answer the resulting question: What then is the ethical meaning, for the ordinary layman in a modern suburb, of being a member of the Christian community?

Because this is such a complex and difficult question, a topic for an entire study on ethics, I have only two suggestions to make to begin the discussion. First, the internal life of the denominational church can no longer merely reflect the fellowship limits of the culture around it, restricted as these limits have been by the same barriers of suburb, class, race, and nation that make our social clubs mere cultural institutions. For then, as the earlier sects realized so well, all holiness of life vanishes from the church and it becomes—what it now often is—merely its own upper-class community in a self-congratulatory and self-righteous pose. The internal fellowship of the church must move toward that of the New Testament koinonia, which knows nothing of cultural or racial barriers. This is the *minimum* requirement if the church is to mediate the holiness of God's law, of His judgment, and of His grace to the world around it. Only thus can it become the holy People of God; only thus can it fulfill the law of its own life and become a community of love.

Second, since the church is *in* secular culture, and all its people actually exist there, the life of the congregation cannot in any sense express transcendence of the culture around it unless it is willing to challenge the injustices and sins of the wider community in which it lives. For a church in culture, especially one that serves the privileged there, there is no alternative: it either criticizes what is evil in the society on which its members feed and prosper, or else, itself implicated, passively accepts and so blesses those evils. Some form of the social gospel is a requirement for a holy church in the world, lest it capitulate entirely to the world and lose its own being. I once, to my astonishment, heard a clergyman say that a church that even discusses social issues has already capitulated to society, since its only function is to shepherd souls to heaven through sacrament or gospel. (Since he was a high Anglican, he opted for the former means, but an evangelical Protestant could have said the same thing in terms of the "gospel alone.") Such views lose sight of the fact that the transcendence of culture is not merely a matter of over-looking social wrongs, especially when the members of this sacramental or gospel-oriented congregation live their entire existence saturated in and fattened from the various privileges, injustices, and coercions that abound in any social order. Only a group which, like the sects, has separated its total existence from society can afford the moral luxury of ignoring that society's structures. Other religious groups that remain within culture profit from those structures, and must therefore be held responsible for their society's moral health or sickness.

What, then, does the social gospel mean for our congregations today? While creative political action where it is clearly needed, as in the racial or disarmament issues, is one aspect of it, certainly the first and most immediate requirement is the freedom to discuss controversial social issues in the churches. Such issues are, we may be sure, already discussed in the locker room and the men's bar; and they are continually weighing on the minds and increasing the anxieties of people in the pews. Should they not also be brought under the Word of God in the congregation? How can our community and national life be brought "under God," as we proudly boast, unless these issues of social policy are debated in the churches? I shall return to this point in the next chapter.

Further, the social gospel today means a careful consideration by members of the congregation of the implications of the gospel for the vocations which they serve in their community. We should encourage our laymen to consider what it means to be a Christian doctor, lawyer, businessman, or citizen. This sort of searching question will enlarge their idea of Christian ethical obligations beyond the narrow limits of personal vice and virtue. It may also be the most fruitful way in which the church can reach out into the world. As we have all learned, it is of little use for the clergy to legislate ethical behavior to the various secular callings of our land; as it is of little use for clergy and other liberals to devise political schemes to resolve such social problems as the costs of medical care, restrictive housing, and so on. It would be far better for those involved in the various vocations to see the Christian ethical responsibility implied in what they do, and in the light of their expert knowledge devise a Christian understanding of their vocational duties. It would not be a bad notion, for that matter, for ministers to inquire as to the *Christian* or even the religious meaning of the increasingly secular vocation of the ministry! In any case, if the laity in the church can catch a glimpse of the Christian meaning and obligation of its daily work in the community, then the denomination, as the free church in the world, may begin to realize some of its great potentialities, transforming rather than being transformed by the world in which it lives.

The symbol of the People of God points to the high moral calling of the church: a calling to be the new community of love, the congregation and fellowship bound together by the Spirit in the bond of peace—a fellowship of reconciliation of all the barriers of men and of churches. Here in this symbol is the deepest root of both the social gospel and the ecumenical movement, and the first and primary task of the church. It is thrilling and inspiring, as a glimpse of the perfection of the law of God always is. But when we see this law for the church's life and then look at ourselves, we can only cry out with the disciples, "How, O Lord, is this impossibility possible?!" And so we must move on to other symbols, symbols of divine grace in and to the church, lest we despair at our continuing betrayal of our own high calling.

4

Hearers of the Word

In the last chapter we looked with some wonder and no little dismay at the first symbol that defines the church in the New Testament. The church is the New Israel of God, the new humanity in Christ, a community characterized by the disappearance of the old barriers and conflicts, privileges and cruelties of sin and ordered into a whole, not by coercion and rank but by mutual love, forbearance, and tolerance. From this we learned first of all that the church can never take itself for granted—as if it were the church merely by setting out to be one, with steeple, preacher, and book. It must always first of all be repentant of its own manifest failures, and militant against the sins in its own existence that deny its life as a community of love. In the face of this symbol, any pride in its own virtue by comparison with the "wicked world" is as absurd as it is incredible. And second, we could not help asking ourselves how such a community of love is possible. Surely such brotherhood is not a natural fact possible for us men, who are sinful? What then is the power that can give life to the dead bones of the church, that can renew it from age to age so that it can *be* the people of God?

In this way we are led inevitably to our second great apostolic symbol or idea: Christ is the Head of the church, and from Him alone it draws power and in Him alone it lives.[1] The apostolic church never based its hope of salvation or acceptability to God on its own holiness or love. It did not, in other words, witness to itself, even as the People of God. Rather it pointed continually beyond itself to its Lord as the sole basis of its faith, trust, and hope in salvation: "For we preach not ourselves but Christ Jesus the Lord."[2] Christ alone is Head of the church, for from Him and not from its own virtue it draws its relationship to God, its full measure of holiness, and so its ability to mediate the holy to men.

The church, then, as the people of the new covenant, is created and recreated by the life, death, resurrection, and continuing lordship of Jesus Christ. It was by this great series of events that the new covenant, and so the new community of the disciples and their converts, was established; and it was the Spirit witnessing to these events that made the new community a living, witnessing fellowship at Pentecost. Thus the church as a community, as the People of God, was constituted by its living knowledge of Jesus Christ and all He means—by Christians' continually reawakened knowledge of Him, and by their response of faith to this knowledge. The Word made flesh in Christ and preached as the Good News in and by the apostolic community is the source and origin of the church.[3] For in the message about Jesus Christ, His life, death, and resurrection, we know in faith of God's establishment of this new humanity; we know the judgment of God on our own sins; we know of His forgiving love, which accepts the repentant into new fellowship; and we know of His promise in the Spirit that in faith we may grow in Christian holiness. Salvation can come to individuals in the community of the church—peace, joy, and love—only through this communication of the Word of Jesus Christ and the response of the community to the Word in faith.

---

[1] Eph. 1:22-23, 5:23-27; Col. 1:18-20.

[2] II Cor. 4:5. See also I Cor. 1:13-15, 2:2-5.

[3] Cf. Paul's ringing assertion that his commission as an apostle, is the "preaching of the gospel of Christ," and that this is the power of God unto salvation, and so the instrument of the calling of men "unto Christ" and into His community, the church: I Cor. 1:17-31, and also Rom. 10:1-18.

This is what the Reformation churches meant when they said that the church is established by the Word of God as the source and norm of its life.[4] For the Word is the message of God's act of salvation in Jesus Christ. This Word became flesh in Jesus, it was witnessed to in Scripture, and it is to be preached ever anew in the life of the community of God. In the course of history since our Lord's time, that community alone has been a living witness to this Word in the reading of Scripture, the preaching from it, and the response of the listening, reading, and seeking congregation that has ever again re-established and reconstituted the continuing covenant community: the congregation—that is, the church. It is by this message that men are personally "called out by God" to form the ecclesia or congregation; and it is by this message in Scripture and preaching that the congregation maintains its living knowledge of its Head, Jesus Christ. In terms of our symbols, the church is formed or constituted by the Word of God's grace and love, and not by the task or law of the church, which is to become the People of God.

[4] The relation in Reformation thought between God's Word, faith, salvation, and the church is clearly stated in the following: "God's Word is the beginning of all; on it follows faith and on faith charity . . . In no other way can man come to God and deal with Him than through faith; that is, not man, by any work of His, but God, by His promise, is the author of salvation, so that all things depend on the word . . . with which He begat us, that we should be a kind of firstfruits of His creatures." "The Babylonian Captivity of the Church," *Works of Martin Luther*, Vol. II (Philadelphia: Muhlenberg, 943), p. 198. "For He Himself said, 'One thing only is necessary' [Luke 10:42], the Word of God, in which man has life. For if he lives in the Word and has the Word, he is able to forego all else in order to avoid the teachings and ministries of impious men." "Concerning the Ministry," *Luther's Works*, J. Pelikan, ed., Vol. 40 (St. Louis, Mo.: Concordia, 1958), p. 10. Thus, "For since the Church owes its birth to the Word, is nourished, aided and strengthened by it, it is obvious that it cannot be without the Word. If it is without the Word, it ceases to be a church." *Ibid.*, p. 37.

Calvin is in complete agreement with Luther on the absolute centrality of the Word for salvation and so for the church: "The same Divine word is the foundation by which faith is sustained and supported, from which it cannot be moved without an immediate downfall. Take away the word, then, and there will be no faith left." John Calvin, *Institutes of the Christian Religion*, trans. by J. Allen, Bk. III, Chap. II, sec. 6 (Philadelphia: Presbyterian Board of Christian Education, 1936), Vol. I, p. 602. This theme is continued in his famous definition of the marks of a true, visible church: "Wherever we find the word of God purely preached and heard, and the

Thus the Word, as preached and read and responded to in faith, is for Protestants the first and primary means by which Jesus Christ relates himself to his community. As the Reformers asserted, it is through the Word that Christ is and becomes the Head of the Church. Let us note further that in this way the Protestant church is in the fullest sense apostolic. For in so far as its life is based on this Word, that life stems solely and continually from the apostolic witness to our Lord, and each historic form of the church's existence is to be measured and tested solely by this norm of the apostolic Word. The continuity of the church with the apostles is established for us, therefore, not through an unbroken line of ecclesiastics with sacramental power, but by fidelity in preaching, teaching, and witness to the message of the apostles in Scripture.

As has been seen in our previous analyses, however, this peculiarly Protestant continuity with Christ through the Word of Scripture and preaching is not a relation which we can take for granted—by maintaining either the purity of our doctrine or the numbers of our quotations from the Bible. For the Word that creates and recreates the church is neither a system of

---

sacraments administered according to the institution of Christ, there, it is not to be doubted, is a Church of God." *Ibid.*, Bk. IV, Chap. I, sec. 9, Vol. II, p. 281. (Note how near to this is Luther's earlier definition of the marks of the visible church: "The external marks, whereby one can perceive where the Church is on earth, are baptism, the sacrament, and the Gospel . . ." "The Papacy at Rome," *Works* [Muhlenberg ed.], Vol. 1, p. 361.). Further, on the spiritual power of the church Calvin says: "Now the only way to edify the Church is, for the ministers to study to preserve to Jesus Christ his rightful authority, which can no longer be secure than while he is left in possession of what he has received from the Father, that is, to be sole Master in the Church. For of him alone, and of no other, is it said, 'Hear ye him . . .' For when they [ministers] were called to their office, it was at the same time enjoined that they should bring forward nothing of themselves, but should speak from the mouth of the Lord. Nor did he send them forth in public to address the people, before he had instructed them what they should say, that they might speak nothing beside his word . . . The power of the Church therefore, is not unlimited, but subject to the word of the Lord, and, as it were included in it . . . Let us lay down this, then, as an undoubted axiom, that nothing ought to be admitted in the Church as the Word of God, but what is contained first in the law and the prophets, and secondly in the writings of the apostles, and that there is no other method of teaching aright in the Church than according to the direction and standard of that word." *Op. cit.*, Bk. IV, Chap. VIII, secs. 1-8, Vol. II, pp. 416-23.

doctrine nor a series of scriptural passages. It is, rather, the living impact of God's revelation in Christ on a community of men: it is the immediate address to a community of God's judgment on their sins; of His forgiveness and love, with which they are received into fellowship again; and of the personal promise of His grace, by which they may live in hope. It is, as I said in Chapter I, the claim of the Lord Jesus on the lives and decisions of the community, to which they can only respond in commitment. Thus the Word is never heard by a living congregation merely in terms of intellectual agreement to a set of traditional dogmas.[5] It is heard and received only by repentance for our own *particular* and *specific* sins, and by the reawakened personal trust, obedience, and dedication of self that true knowledge of Jesus Christ always brings. Again, the reality of the Word of God in the congregation, and so the transcendence of the source and norm of its life, depends utterly on the relevance to the actual life of the congregation with which that Word is preached and taught. The trait of "orthodoxy" in any doctrine, without

[5] Luther and Calvin are in harmony on this further point, namely that the Word is heard not by a mere assent to dogma, but when the living impact of God's judgment and promise is felt in the heart of the believer. For both writers this is the significance of the theme of the Holy Spirit, illumining the heart so that it hears the Word, and of their "existential" character when they write about the Word of God and the response of faith. Illustrative quotations abound in both; the following may be taken as typical: "But weigh diligently every word of Paul, and specially mark well this pronoun 'our'; for the effect altogether consisteth in the well applying of the pronouns, which we find very often in the scriptures; wherein also there is ever some vehemency and power. Thou wilt easily say and believe that Christ the Son of God was given for the sins of Peter, of Paul, and of other saints, whom we account to have been worthy of this grace; but it is a very hard thing that thou which judgest thyself unworthy of this grace, shouldst from thy heart say and believe that Christ was given for thine invincible, infinite, and horrible sins . . . But when it cometh to the putting of this pronoun 'our,' there our weak nature and reason starteth back, and dare not come near unto God, nor promise to himself that so great a treasure shall be freely given unto her . . . And except thou be found in the number of those that say 'our sins,' that is, which have this doctrine of faith, and teach, hear, learn, love and believe the same, there is no salvation for thee." Martin Luther, *A Commentary on St. Paul's Epistle to the Galatians* (Westwood, N.J.: Revell, 1953), pp. 48-49.

And from Calvin: "Cold and frivolous, then, are the speculations of those who employ themselves in disquisitions on the essence of God, when it would be more interesting to us to become acquainted with his character, and to know what is agreeable to his nature . . . What benefit arises from

the corresponding trait of relevance, will by itself never bring the transcendent Word into the church.

Now this reveals to us the truly awesome task of the minister as preacher, teacher, and pastor.[6] It is his vocation and commission to mediate this living Word to his congregation: to lead it through his preaching and counsel to become aware of this claim of our Lord—to discover God's judgment, mercy, and love, which come to us through the apostolic witness in Scripture. This is an awesome task, and every good minister realizes that he cannot possibly fulfill it merely through his own powers; that no amount of anecdotes, clever titles, or brilliance of oratory can communicate the important thing: the judgment and love of God. All they can communicate is his own ego, and that will not feed his congregation. Only by a deep understanding of his commission to be a servant of the Word and of Scripture—by fidelity to this task, whether it leads to popularity or unpopularity (and often the former is more dangerous),[7] and by a continual listening in his personal life for the claim the Lord Jesus makes upon him and his congregation through Scripture—can he perform this task.

---

the knowledge of a God with whom we have no concern? Our knowledge of God should rather tend, first, to teach us fear and reverence; and second, to instruct us to implore all good at his hand, and to render him the praise of all that we receive." Thus he goes on to say that the true knowledge of God leads inevitably to "true religion." *Op. cit.*, Bk. I, Chap. II, sec. 2, Vol. I, pp. 52-53. In the case of both Reformation traditions, however, the polar emphasis on "right doctrine" which we have already noted triumphed over the "existential" emphasis on the appropriation of the Word in the Spirit, with the result that soon "hearing the Word" implied listening to correct doctrine rather than this more immediate, personal meaning.

[6] "The public ministry of the Word, I hold, by which the mysteries of God are made known, ought to be established by holy ordination as the highest and greatest of the functions of the Church, on which the whole power of the Church depends, since the Church is nothing without the Word and everything in it exists by virtue of the Word alone." Luther, "Concerning the Ministry," *op. cit.*, p. 11.

[7] See Luther's warning on the dangers of popularity: "I know many preachers who stand there and preach cheerfully. Their teaching has many adherents; that is why they preach so cheerfully. But if their hearers fell away from their teaching, they would stop preaching and fall away from their teaching themselves. Their heart is not in it. They mention Christ's name with their mouth, but they do not mean it . . . If you can dispense with popularity, honor, support, and acceptance, that is good. But it is innate in us and it clings to us that we want to have people like us, and when

And it is an essential task: for if the Word is not heard in the church—if, as is so often the case, only the prejudices and ideologies of the world, or the thoughts, however noble, of the minister are heard there—then this tie with Christ, the Head of the church, is broken and the church slips back into the world to become nothing more than the world. For in Protestantism the central mediation of the holy in the life of the church comes through the Word, the message of Jesus Christ in lordly claim, in judgment, and in grace. If, as we have seen, this message is not heard, believed, and enacted, then the main element of holiness in the Protestant church is gone, and it reflects merely the views and ideals of its surrounding society. It voices only the thoughts that all American middle-class white groups have; it has conformed to the world and has lost its Lord. Its Head has become, not the Lord Jesus, but the popular self-image of the average American man and woman—and there is some difference.

We can see this denial of Christ and this subservience to the surrounding world very clearly in other countries where the churches seek to exist under other forms of government than our own, for example, behind the Iron Curtain. We are very conscious of the betrayal of Christ, if from the pulpits of those churches we hear nothing but Communist ideology preached because of public and private pressures on the preacher. And we ask ourselves wonderingly how in that situation a true servant of God could refrain from crying out in the name of the Word and its Lord against the tyranny, the oppression, and the slave labor of those Communist countries.

Should we not, however, also look at our American churches, in North and South alike? How often do we hear their voices raised in moral questioning of our international policy? "Oh no," we are apt to say. "This is a matter of national security!" How often did we hear the question of personal freedoms raised in the churches when the recent congressional investigations were in

---

they stop liking us, that bothers us. This truly shows that the heart is impure . . . He lets himself be tickled by the shaft of the ministry. He turns his eyes away from the divine Word to his own pleasure, and he does not say as does David here, "Only winnow me thoroughly." "Psalm 26," commentary, *Works* (Pelikan ed.), Vol. 12, pp. 190-91.

full cry? "Oh no," we say. "That's politics, not religion!" How often are our racial patterns discussed seriously and prayerfully in the church in the light of God's Word? "Oh no," we say. "Such discussions might split the church, so little do our people want them!" The word that is heard there is often either an irrelevant, unrelated "gospel" that heals no one because it sears no one, or merely the accepted wisdom of the world, untransformed by any transcendent judging and healing elements, and therefore also ultimately sterile. How life can be made more serene and peaceful, how to deal with our worries, how to be a success, how to make adjustments—the wisdom of the public relations man, the psychoanalyst, or the village philosopher. But neither individual nor community will be transformed, inwardly or in important external relationships, by the world's wisdom.

This is perhaps the final commission of the minister: that within his human words and human wisdom there be the possibility of the divine Word. He cannot himself make his words divine. But by being faithful to the gospel and the Scripture as he reads them, and by making sure that his preaching is relevant to the actual moral life and moral decisions of his community, he may through grace become a channel of God's Word to those among whom he labors. A man was overheard to say about a ministerial colleague of ours several years ago in Nashville, "Oh, he couldn't take a stand on that subject in his preaching—you see, he hopes to be a bishop." And the tragedy is that the layman who made the remark apparently had no criticism of the clergyman in question. It was how any wise minister who wanted to move up into a bishop's position or a larger church would naturally act. Is this, then, the relation of the minister to the Word in our churches? And if so, does the church have any chance to hear the Word? If this is the relation, then Protestantism is in real danger. Since in Protestantism there are no other separated media of God's holiness, this absence of the Word of God means that the church has lost its touch with the holy, with the Christ who is its Lord.

We may ask, further, how we can find the will of God for our corporate life if in the churches we do not earnestly seek His will for our social existence, through preaching and discussion of our corporate problems. Often we address ourselves to vices that do not trouble our own congregation, and avoid all the great moral problems that face us as a community: issues of national policy (nuclear armament and disarmament, aggression or nonaggression in Cuba), issues of political corruption, race relations, economic justice, all the unadmitted causes of personal anxiety in the congregation's life, and questions of personal morals where they characteristically fall short (for example, padded expense accounts and other peculiarly suburban vices). If these actual problems are not raised in the congregation, in the light of God's law and His Word to us of judgment, love, and forgiveness, then where and how can they be resolved in a Christian way by Christian men? They are thought about, argued, worried over, and decided somewhere—at service club luncheons, in suburban living rooms, in country club locker rooms and porches. We Americans proclaim ourselves to be a nation "under God." Let us remember that unless the community of the church seeks the divine will and declares its mind—repentantly and humbly, but firmly—on all these great problems of our common life, there is no way on earth that the common life of the nation can be brought under God. The Word of God to community, nation, and world can come to it only if the church is faithful to its task and its Lord and declares His Word in the congregation.

I do not mean that either church or minister can have pat or definitive answers to the great moral problems of our age. But if a Christian answer is to be found to these problems, it must be found in relation to the will of God, and each of us can find the will of God for us as a community much more soundly in the fellowship of the church than in the loneliness of our own souls. The church is, therefore, not only a congregation hearing the Word from its minister, but also a community of Christians seeking responsibly and seriously together for the Word of God in the most pressing problems before them. The preaching of the minister should be the beginning, not necessarily the end, of discussion. It is surely his duty first to declare his understanding of the Word of God in Scripture on the great issues of our time; second, to teach the stand of the wider church, denominational and national, on these issues; and third, to raise all the important moral problems he feels to be evident in them, as well as providing whatever enlightening technical material he can obtain. But the task is ultimately one for the whole congregation, namely, under the leadership of the minister, and in relation to Scripture, to find the will of God through His Word. This in turn is the essence and glory of our congregational tradition in the church: that in seeking God's will and listening to his Word, we do so as a community of hearers of that Word.[8] Let us as ministers remember that our congregations have no chance to become real *congregations* in this deeper sense, as communities of personal, individual repentance and faith, unless we have the courage to raise these issues and the perseverance to discuss them among our people.

We have seen, then, how crucial to the holiness, the transcendence, and the relevance of the Protestant churches is the authority of the Word of God. Our question now is: In the light of the present denominational situation, with lay-centered churches

[8] For the early Luther (1523) the priesthood of all believers includes the necessity of all to know and believe the Word by and for themselves; *each* must then be a hearer and judge of the Word for himself: "What else does this mean than that each of us shall have regard for his own salvation and be sure of Him in whom He believes and whom He follows? Each is a most free judge of all who teach him, if he himself is inwardly taught of God . . . For you will not be damned or saved by the teaching of another, be it true or false, but by your faith alone. Anyone may teach as he pleases, but what you believe is your responsibility whether it result in your peril or benefit." "Concerning the Ministry," *op. cit.*, p. 32. Thus, as true hearers of the Word, *each* Christian is also called to proclaim the Word: "The first office, that of the ministry of the Word, therefore, is common to all Christians . . . And Peter not only gives them the right, but the command, to declare the wonderful deeds of God, which is certainly nothing else than to preach the Word of God." *Ibid.*, pp. 21-22. Later, as he became fearful of Anabaptist excesses and more concerned with right doctrine, he came to emphasize the sole authority of a clerical office to declare "the external meaning of the Word," i.e., its doctrinal as opposed to its existential meaning; and this new emphasis rather snuffed out his early conviction that all members of the congregation were recipients and so declarers of the Word. "The second is an external judgment. By it we judge the spirits and doctrines of all men, also with the greatest certainty, and not now for ourselves only, but also for the benefit and salvation of others. This judgment is the province of the public ministry of the Word and the external office, and is the special concern of teachers and preachers of the Word." Luther, *The Bondage of the Will*, trans. by J. I. Packer and O. R. Johnston (Westwood, N.J.: Revell, 1957), III, 3, p. 125.

in culture, how can this authority of the Word in the church be maintained? How can Jesus Christ become Lord of His church amongst *us?* Certainly to specify any human conditions for the lordship of Christ is presumptuous indeed, but we are called to think about our problems and to do what we can in His service.

First of all we need a new and higher view of the function of the minister in the congregation. In the older sectarian groups the notion that the clergyman was a trained man who spoke with authority on biblical, theological, and ethical subjects tended to disappear. The whole congregation was assumed to be equally learned in, and committed to, the faith. However, when the church becomes coextensive with the world, when its members receive their dominant ideas—religious and ethical —from their business life, from service club speakers, and from weekly magazines, then a new situation has arisen for authority in the church. Now the voice of the layman reflects in all probability the simple voice of his culture. In this case, if the authority of the minister is felt to arise solely from the congregation and his function is understood to be solely that of serving their needs and meeting their standards, then pulpit and church alike are apt to be less free than under an ecclesiastical hierarchy—as the recent integration of Catholic schools in New Orleans has so vividly shown us.

Protestantism should seek in our day to recapture its older tradition: that the pulpit, he who stands in it, and so the church as a whole, are first of all servants of the Word, not of the mind of the congregation. It should be emphasized that it is the minister's task and duty to bring the judgment of God as well as the comforts of His grace upon the congregation and its life —especially where they least expect and wish it. Protestantism unseated the pope, not in order to replace him by the congregation, but to enthrone Jesus Christ, the Word of God, there.

Let us note that this higher status of the minister in the congregation is not merely a matter of polity. For Methodist and Presbyterian ministers can find themselves in difficulties with their congregations as well as can Disciples and Baptists—though perhaps not quite so often. It is rather a matter of the understanding of the role, function, and authority of the minister.

American Protestantism has separated him from the congregation at just the wrong point. We expect him to follow a higher and more saintly moral code, but give him little theological or ethical authority in preaching or in the discussions of the church. Before he is a saint, however, he is first of all the servant of the Word and the representative of the wider church in the midst of his congregation. His responsibility, then, for the salvation and guidance of his people is not to cater to their wishes but to disclose forthrightly what, to him, the Word declares on pertinent issues of their life, and what the church has taught on these issues. And we should add, as the Reformers did, that the minister is responsible to hear criticism and objection to what he says solely on the basis of Scripture and the wider tradition of the church, and to allow no silencing of these declarations on the grounds of local custom, congregational wishes, or the problem of splitting the church. It is best of all when, through his preaching, the congregation as a whole is led to search the Scriptures and the wisdom of the wider church for its guidance on real and pressing problems. Then is the Word the real authority in the church, even in the midst of suburbia.

Second, if the congregation is to hear and obey the Word in its midst, the denominational church must lose its fear of and scorn for theology, and its resistance to the teaching of doctrine in the church. The life of historic American Protestantism has been based on the familiarity of the Bible to the congregation and the intelligibility and convincingness of its message to their several minds. Only thus has free-church Protestantism been able to dispense with creedal and theological requirements, and incidentally to free the mind to accept culture.

To the religiously untutored layman *in* modern culture, however, dominated as his thinking is by the causal order and worldly values of modern commercial and secular society, the Bible seems a strange, unbelievable, and largely irrelevant piece of writing. In the "real" world of commercial and technological life all happens by natural law, values are created by human effort, and he who looks after himself usually prospers. In the biblical world, on the contrary, most events seem to be the work of supernatural powers, man is portrayed as in desperate need of an invisible and intangible grace, and he who seeks his life will surely lose it. What, then, is modern man, conservative or liberal, honestly to make of this document, which seems so incompatible with what he knows of natural causality, and so opposite to all he values? How can he simply regard it as "true"? The Bible, as one person frankly admitted to me, pictures a Never-Never Land of miracles and wonders, as far removed from Nashville, Tennessee, as the moon, and (he worriedly owned up) fortunately so. "I couldn't last a minute as a businessman if I followed its precepts to take no thought for the morrow and trust God alone in all things!" No wonder those who "know their Bibles" in our conservative churches know only incidents, names, and numbers in the Book, and not its great religious themes; for such incidents, names, and numbers raise no problems to the modern mind of the *truth* in principle of Scripture, whereas the themes surely do. Because, therefore, the Bible is to modern churchmen such a strange and alien document, they have ceased to read it seriously or to become genuinely acquainted with its contents.[9] It is a book seen in every churchman's living room but little used, and surely not the prevailing source of their picture of the real world, as it used to be. The message of the Bible is known only dimly in the churches: a series of vague

[9] Several years of Sunday school teaching in a Nashville church, and the frequent researches of students into the religious habits, capacities, interests, and learning of their parishioners, long ago convinced the writer that even in the "Bible Belt" the Bible is a relatively unknown book—sacred, of course, but quite unfamiliar. This impression was more than validated by Obenhaus and Schroeder's fascinating study of church life in Illinois. On this score they have the following to say: "It might be hypothesized, therefore, that church people with so substantial a background of Biblical emphasis would be reasonably well informed about major ideas, personalities, and the implications of the Bible for the life of people today. As was true of some previously expressed hypotheses, the findings do not support this one either . . . a low level of comprehension of Biblical meanings characterizes all denominations of Corn County regardless of education or degree of Biblical studies." Victor Obenhaus, *The Church and Faith in Mid-America* (Philadelphia: Westminster Press, 1963), p. 72. They found that "63 per cent of the Protestants indicate no knowledge of any difference (between Old and New Testaments)" (p. 74); that "more than half the Presbyterian and Congregational members had no knowledge of the Old Testament prophets. In their uniformedness they are exceeded slightly by the Methodists, United Lutheran, Augustania Lutheran, and Disciples" (p. 77); "to discover that less than one-third of their people find in the good Samaritan parable an admonition to provide aid to others, or to express it another way, to learn that more than a third of their people had no idea of any meaning

concepts of God, man, and salvation which, because they are so very vague, can be given whatever content the culture may wish to provide. The main result of this contemporary unintelligibility of the Scriptures and consequent unfamiliarity of their contents, is that the biblical doctrines preached and spoken in the churches have ceased to carry any real ring of truth or concern to the layman. They hang in the air as appropriate words and phrases for use on Sunday, but are seldom taken as guides to a deeper and truer understanding of the real nature of life. In fact, the church ceases to be valued as the medium of holy truth.[10]

Why is the church valued, as it clearly is, in our contemporary society? Is it because, as in the early church, people are convinced that it bears the *truth* about reality—that its message about God, the cosmos, and man is the key to the way things really are, and therefore we have to do here with the ultimately real world, more real by far than the day-to-day world of business and commerce, of dogs and children, of movies and a friendly drink on the back patio? Such is at any rate not my experience.

The church is loved and supported in our society for a number of other reasons quite unrelated to the truth or relevance of its message. These grounds for its current popularity are, I suspect,

---

that might be attached to the parable would probably be a source of consternation to the Methodist, the United Lutherans, and the Congregationalists" (p. 79). It may be taken as established, therefore, that for all practical purposes the Bible is an unknown book to our congregations, and the phrases "a Bible people" or "a biblical church" have little real meaning if applied to any of our larger free-church denominations.

[10] One can only with some dismay compare our present situation, where the "truth" which the church proclaims is unknown and ignored, with the earlier view of the church as the bearer of Holy Truth, e.g., in Irenaeus, A.D. c. 140-90: "But the preaching of the church is everywhere consistent, and continues in an even course and receives testimony from the prophets, the apostles and all the Disciples . . . through the entire dispensation of God, and that well-grounded system which tends to man's salvation, namely our faith; which, having been received from the church, we do preserve, and which always, by the Spirit of God, renewing its youth, as if it were some precious deposit in an excellent vessel, causes the vessel itself containing it to renew its youth also. For this gift of God has been entrusted to the Church, as breath was to the first created man, for this purpose, that all the members receiving it may be vivified." Irenaeus, *Against Heresies*, Bk. III, Chap. XXIV, sec. 1, found in *The Ante-Nicene Fathers*, Vol. I, (Grand Rapids, Mich.: Eerdmans, 1950), p. 458.

three. First, it is supported because it represents in institutional form the serious, responsible, moral life of our communities. Thus a young couple who do not wish their lives to be (in their own eyes as well as others') irresponsible, unserious, unwilling to help the worthwhile things, joins the church. Their purpose is to give moral and responsible structure and serious meaning to their lives in their own estimate of themselves. They feel better, more stable, more creative and responsible, when they are active within this clearly most worthwhile of society's institutions.

Second, the church is valued because it provides moral and spiritual tutelage for society. This is less a matter of the truth of what is taught there, about which parents are surprisingly little concerned, as that children there go through an education, so to speak, in moral and spiritual things. It is, in the deeper dimensions of life, roughly the equivalent of what good grooming accomplishes in etiquette. Through the church, that is to say, our children are brought from barbarism into civilization. Sunday school for the kids is, for many active young parents, not only the main basis of their personal interest in church (modern worship must be set when the children are brought to school, so that parents will also come), but under pressure it is admitted to be for them its main social importance. In both aspects, let us note, the church has a significant but strictly cultural function as an institution by which the moral and spiritual values of the community (its "way of life," as we now put it) are preserved and transmitted. There are many reasons why the modern denominational church can truly be called "established," but among them all this is the deepest: it is an integral factor in the stability and continuity of our cultural life.[11]

[11] In his book on the church as a human community, already cited, Gustafson points to this natural function of the church as a culturally integrating and educative institution: "The Church, like other societies, is an agent of socialization; persons absorb socially acceptable values within the life of the Christian community. The Church participates in processes common to all human communities as it maintains its social and historical identity; it must have adequate ways to transmit its cultural heritage, or to control aberrant behaviour within the community." James Gustafson, *Treasure in Earthen Vessels* (New York: Harper & Row, 1961), p. 15. While there is no doubt, as Gustafson says, that this purely social function of cultural transmission is not only natural but valuable, it is another matter if these natural and cultural functions of the church quite eclipse the religious functions that are more peculiarly its own.

Third, as the sociologists and psychologists rightly assure us, the church, located in the exclusive suburb, provides a warm fellowship of peers in an urban existence which in its ordinary course offers nothing but external, utilitarian, and contractual relations.[12] Through its endless and often religiously meaningless activities, people come to feel that they "belong" to a community in a world where such feelings are rare.[13] It is thus (as is so often said in our churches) the "church home" for families of two or three who, without such a wider "family" group, are too much alone in the vastness and impersonality of modern society. Again the church fulfills an important but purely cultural role, offering a close fellowship of equals in a society devoid of such communities.

What is significant for our immediate purposes in these reasons for present church growth and success is that the church as the bearer of truth seldom if ever functions here. One never hears this value mentioned, and the reason is not too difficult to discover. Most churches, and most laymen in them, have been content to leave the beliefs or doctrines of the church right

[12] Cf. Winter: "Impersonality in work and exchange is taken for granted in contemporary society . . . The extensive development of metropolitan life depends principally upon impersonal interdependence . . ." Gibson Winter, *The Suburban Captivity of the Churches* (Garden City, L.I.: Doubleday & Co., 1961), p. 22. "The residential community strives for stability by insulating itself against contacts with social differences which the interdependent metropolis overlooks . . . The open market and the insulated neighborhood represent the two types of metropolitan organization—impersonal interdependence and insulated, communal solidarity, inclusiveness and exclusiveness, common humanity and social differences." *Ibid.*, p. 23. And finally, the consequence is that the church, which is organized around these isolated, insulated residential neighborhoods, is concerned only with the private, personal, emotional affairs of its exclusive suburban family contacts: "Religious faith and practice have become a private sphere of American life—a sphere preoccupied with the emotional balance of the membership, the nurture of children, and the preservation of a harmonious residential milieu . . . The inevitable consequence is social irresponsibility, which means that the churches have abandoned a context of public accountability in order to serve exclusively the emotional needs of selected groups . . ." *Ibid.*, pp. 134-35.

The only qualification the author has to this thesis is that the drive toward a "homogeneous society of peers" in the suburban churches takes place in smaller urban centers, such as Nashville, as manifestly as it does in large cities such as Detroit or Chicago. Since, however, the "life downtown" in these smaller cities is by no means socially heterogeneous, most of the men who do business with one another being school- and college-mates

where they were fifty years ago, untouched by modern culture
and unchanged by the impact of science. Now, at midcentury,
these beliefs are quite out of touch with the assumptions about
the world that guide our modern cultural life. Close questioning
of the contemporary middle-class layman reveals that he is far
too much influenced by the assumptions of modern technology
and commercialism really to believe that the simple picture of
reality presented to him in these old-time doctrines is *true*.
In so far as he knows what they are or thinks about them at all,
the layman seems to conceive of biblical doctrines as part of
the necessary paraphernalia of the church, to be revered because
they are, so to speak, the flags this valuable institution flies and
because they have been hallowed by his parents and grandparents,
who had "real religion." But while to his rural parents, uneducated in modern science and unsophisticated in their social and
moral existence, this biblical world of miracles was real, sin a
vivid experience, salvation an overwhelming emotional event,
and heaven up there very close—all this is to their smooth,
suburban businessman-son both vague and important, sacrosanct
and utterly unreal.[14] One cannot help but perceive that he does

and now neighbors in the suburbs, apparently churchly homogeneity needs
no further causes than its own obvious pleasures plus slight doses of snob-
bism—it need not be caused by a weekday experience of metropolitan
heterogeneity.

Gustafson offers a slightly different explanation of this drive toward
homogeneity in our urban and suburban churches: "The notion dominant
in American Protestantism that the urban congregation ought to be shaped
by the image of the socially homogeneous rural congregation of a more
stable society indicates the extent to which the foundation of social integration is accepted." *Op. cit.*, p. 25.

[13] Again Winter describes this function of the church and its activities:
"The round of activities in the organization church is a celebration of its
own unity through which some sense of community is evoked." *Op. cit.*,
p. 96.

[14] Winter rightly points out in a fascinating section that the emphasis on
activity as opposed to belief (the category of truth) in the church is part
of the universal activism of our middle-class society: "The clue to the religious significance of this organizational membership is provided by its ac-
tivistic style, which emphasized external criteria of performance as a basis of
evaluation: not how you *feel* or what you *believe* but what you *do*. The
good church member is one who *does* things: *works* on this, accomplishes
that . . . The search for meaning through activity and performance is
typically middle-class. To be a successful middle-class person is to perform
adequately." *Ibid.*, p. 100. While this is certainly true, it is not, I believe, the

not think they are true. However conservative the contemporary Texas Baptist layman may be as to the literal truth of biblical dogmas, he still calls the geologist and not the preacher when he wants to find oil, though he will insist in church on the old-time doctrines that clearly exclude the geology he really *knows* to be fact.

What we face, in other words, is the loss of the category of truth as a relevant one in our modern denominational life, and this loss is, strangely, a greater danger for our conservative brethren than among the liberals, who have at least sought to make their gospel intelligible in terms of the modern layman's world. Such a loss, if fully realized, would of course be fatal to the Protestant character of our denominational life, and ultimately to its moral and spiritual strength. Protestantism can exist as a vital form of religion only on the twin assumptions of the presence of the Word of God in the church and the priesthood of all believers. The latter, which is our immediate concern here, implies that each man believes this Word of God—the gospel—for himself and of himself.[15] And such personal, inner belief requires that a man find the doctrines of his religion convincing to his

---

whole story. Some beliefs are still regarded as of supreme importance by modern suburban residents—beliefs, that is, about things that "matter": laissez-faire economics, the evils of socialized medicine, creeping socialism, and the dangers of Communism and Cuba. In this *real* world of commerce, politics, and society beliefs are as important as they ever were, and correspondingly, *in these vital areas* people are as much evaluated according to their beliefs as they were in religious matters two hundred years ago. One is led to suggest that the contemporary unimportance of belief in the church is due to the secularization of the Western mind, to the consequent unintelligibility of biblical and/or Christian doctrine to those untrained in these matters, and so, finally, to the ordinary man's total ignorance of and indifference to the ideas and beliefs appearing in the life of the church. The bourgeoisie, in its history since the sixteenth century, has had its own significant intellectual tradition and systems of belief, to which it has held with great passion (among these systems of belief, as Weber and Tillich have pointed out, have been the "doctrinal religions" of the Reformation). Without such deeply held and frequently well-thought-out beliefs on the part of the bourgeoisie, our modern scientific and democratic culture would not have been possible.

[15] This need on the part of every man that he believe "for himself" was expressed often by Luther, but nowhere with more characteristic vigor than in the following: "The challenge of death comes to us all, and no one can die for another. Everyone must fight his own battle with death by himself, alone. We can shout into one another's ears, but everyone must be prepared

own mind and intelligible in terms of all else he knows to be true. Only under those conditions can it be said that a belief is *true* for a man, and only if he both understands it and believes it to be true can he declare that faith, as a priest might do, to his neighbor. If, as seems now to be occurring, the laity ceases to be concerned about the content or truth of the Christian message: that God is, that He is the Creator, Ruler, Judge, and Redeemer through Jesus Christ, that He has called us to faith and love, and so on—if the churchman regards all this as "theology" known only to preachers, or responds to questions of belief merely, as one man did when the query was put to him, by "Ask Frank, our preacher; he's the expert on beliefs here" (yet he *knew* what he believed about important things such as the TVA, Cuba, integration, medicare, and so forth)—if, in this way, the laity ceases to care about the truth of Christianity, then Protestantism in its historical form is surely dying or already dead.[16] For in that case only the trained clergy know the faith, understand it, and so believe it, as in medieval times; and the holiness of the church,

---

finally to meet death alone. I will not be with you then, nor you with me. Therefore everyone must know for himself the chief things in Christianity, and be armed therewith." First Wittenberg sermon (1522), in "Eight Sermons by Dr. Martin Luther," *Works* (Muhlenberg ed.), Vol. II, p. 391.

[16] That the situation with regard to either acquaintance with or understanding of the essentials of Christian belief is very serious, Obenhaus' study amply shows. As to the simplest Christian concepts most laymen seemed either totally ignorant or quite unable to form any consistent cluster of ideas. In response to such a simple question as, "If a child should ask you what is God like, what would you say?" for example, the authors found: "Few seemed to have given much thought to the nature of this being and even fewer have attempted to formulate their thoughts in any consistent fashion," and again, "an almost complete avoidance of any suggestion that God presented a judgmental aspect may be worthy of investigation." Obenhaus, *op. cit.*, pp. 152-53.

The seriousness of this almost total lack of comprehension of biblical and theological symbols on the part of most churchmen is strongly brought out by Gustafson's emphasis that, sociologically considered, a community can only maintain its identity and character if its members share a commonly understood and so "internalized" system of symbols, in this case the biblical symbols. "Belonging to the Christian community means having its common language. The Church is a community because communication within it occurs through common symbols." *Op. cit.*, p. 10. "Like all human communities, the Church engages in processes of communication through the verbal symbols that are peculiarly its own" (p. 42), and "The community of Christians maintains its social identity and inner unity through the in-here as in the ethical realm, resides solely amongst them. Such a two-level faith may be viable for a dogmatic and sacramental form of religion such as Catholicism, but it is surely hopeless in a lay-centered, voluntary, personal, and inward faith such as Protestant denominationalism. If the Word is to be an authority in our churches, then that Word must be understood and believed to be the truth about life and reality, not only by the minister who preaches, but just as much by the congregation who hear.

It would be wrong, however, to imply that this theological vacuum in our churches is only the fault of the secularization and consequent indifference of the laity. Manifestly it is also the fault of the clergy and whoever among their teachers has given them advice. By their seminary training in the modern understanding of the Bible, in philosophy of religion, and in theology the clergy know well that the church has long since abandoned its older beliefs in an infallible Scripture, a miraculous world order, and a simple, literal understanding of Christian doctrine (a six-day creation, ascension in space, and so on), which dominated evangelical Christianity. When ministers talk among themselves there is a tacit understanding that neither the Bible nor Christian doctrines conflict with the new world of science, even though they may not feel able themselves to spell out a symbolic theology that can put the two worlds together. But do they announce this good news to their intelligent laity; do they tell them that it is now possible honestly to believe, as they themselves do, both

---

ternalization of meanings represented objectively in certain documents, symbols and rites" (p. 43). "Identity in history and across cultures depends upon the internalization of meanings carried potentially in these objects" (p. 48); and finally, "The Church's social identity depends, then, upon two-fold process: the continued use of the Biblical language within the common life of the Church, and its use in interpreting and understanding general human experience as it exists outside the Church" (p. 51). If, as Gustafson maintains, the church can survive only when its members share a comprehended and internalized set of biblical symbols, then empirical study of the church reveals it as a seriously sick institution! My only quarrel with this excellent book is that, while he carefully avoids deducing the nature of the church from purely theological and biblical symbols, Gustafson is inclined to deduce its characteristic traits from sociological conceptions of community—and, as the above excerpts show, this method may also present a somewhat theoretical and "nonempirical" picture of the church.

in the validity of modern science and in the truth of the Bible
and of central Christian concepts? Despite the fact that this is a
major problem for all modern Christian laymen, as earlier for
each of the clergy personally, in general the ministry maintains
a conspiracy of silence on the subject of biblical criticism and
the relation between Christian concepts and science.

The reasons for this suicidal stillness are many. Certainly the
worst is the fear of controversy and of alienating loyal sup-
porters. The chances are that both laity and ministers are afraid
of raising these issues, each with the other, each believing that the
other, being "conservative" in viewpoint, will be shocked that
such questions should even be broached. My own guess is that
both sides would be immensely relieved if each admitted to the
other that he wished, in his religion as in his daily life, to live in
the modern world, and so to criticize and rethink all the major
doctrines for which the church has traditionally stood.

Whatever the reasons for this conspiracy of silence, the result
in the actual life of many churches is another form of two-level
Christian life: one a level of knowledge or gnosis for the clergy,
where the new historical view of the Bible and the new symbolic
conception of doctrines are recognized and absorbed; the other a
simpler level of "faith," where the Bible is held to be more or less
infallible and Christian doctrines are viewed as literal truths about
simply discernible reality.[17] While such a distinction between the
learned clergy and the ignorant, simple believer may have oper-
ated satisfactorily in past history, when the clergy alone were
educated, today it is quite fatal. And this is precisely because the
layman, even more than the minister, lives consciously in a world

[17] The theology of early Alexandria reflected very much the same split
between the educated minority and the uneducated majority, between the
"Christian Gnostic" on the one hand and the "man of mere faith" on the
other. The difference from our own situation is, of course, that in Alexandria the Gnostic class was the sole group in touch with the science and
philosophies of the culture round about, so that the "uneducated" could remain quite content with their simple faith. As I have suggested, however,
the word "uneducated" hardly applies to the modern layman in any respect
except his religion—thus his religious beliefs become for him irrelevant,
dreamy, and untrue. For a description of the Alexandrian "split-level"
church, cf. Clement of Alexandria, *Miscellanies (Stromateis)*, Book VII,
found in *Alexandrian Christianity*, Henry Chadwick, ed., and J. B. Mayer,
trans., Library of Christian Classics, Vol. II (Philadelphia: Westminster
Press, 1954), especially Chaps. III, VII, X, and XII.

of modern science and technology and absorbs all its secular implications. The fact that he identifies Christian belief with older, fundamentalist notions does *not* mean that he believes this simple faith and rejects the scientific, technological world in which he lives and works—as might have been the case in third-century Alexandria. Rather, the identification of Christian belief with fundamentalism means that these doctrines enter his mind not as true statements about the real world, but as unreal and meaningless slogans somehow connected with a church which for quite other reasons he values and supports.

In any case, there is a good deal of evidence that the reasons given above for the current success of the churches are the real ones: namely, that they provide social and moral stability, but not truth, to people of our day. If so, the church is in a very weak position, for other views of life—for example, that of ethical humanism—may provide a workable moral and social stability without having to depend on a transcendent dimension, as does the historic Christian faith. And if our churches are valued merely for their cultural effects and not for the truth they bear, religion will be dispensed with the moment another view seems to give the same social results without the socially useless and often culturally incredible incubus of doctrine.[18]

[18] Obenhaus poses much the same query about the future of the church: "The further question has to be asked,—whether it can always be assumed in the future that the basic intent of the life of the church will be given adequate expression in community life unless its people are familiar with the imperatives that lie within the faith . . . One cannot but ask whether a generation that is unfamiliar with the Hebrew prophets . . . can have confidence that prophetic traditions will play any part in social decisions and community welfare of the next generation.

"The fact that each denomination presented a similar degree of unfamiliarity with the Biblical foundations and their relevance for the contemporary scene can but lead to the conclusion that (1) other forces have minimized, diluted or rendered meaningless the Biblical insights as they pertain to society, or (2) ministerial leadership has been unwilling or unable to make clear the relationship between religious life and community responsibility." *Op. cit.*, p. 155.

Gustafson also insists that a church that has lost touch with the meaning of the biblical symbols has almost lost its "soul": "Though other important symbols exist in the life of the Church, language remains the socially most important mode of communication. The particular language of the Church is the language of the Bible. Without familiarity with the Bible (or literature derived from the Bible) through speech and reading, the identity of the Church would not be historically maintained." *Op. cit.*, p. 46.

Finally, no man will recognize the authority of a gospel he no longer regards as true. If we hold to Christianity solely for reasons of social stability, then surely we shall reject it whenever it threatens the way of life we are unconsciously seeking to preserve. Such religion has only a borrowed authority, derived from the social system it serves. Clearly it can never generate either the real authority or the transcendence necessary for any sort of prophetic criticism of its own social base. Because of this shift in ultimate authority the Methodist laymen quoted earlier were prompted to say, "We don't want to leave the church, but we shall have to if they persist with integration." For such nominal churchmen the real world is that of Southern society, into which their church neatly fits. The real world is not that of God and His judgment, whose truth their church bears—or these Christians, like those of Cyprian's time, would fear for their immortal souls in willingly spurning it. Their error, in other words, is not merely ethical; it is also theological. It is that, like the rest of us, they often do not believe the Word of God to be the *truth*, a truth that concerns the real world in which we live and that we defy at our peril.

What is needed here—and desperately, if the Bible is to be any sort of authority in the church—is theological mediation. By theology I mean the effort to understand the Word of God in our own terms in relation to all else we assume to be true and believe to be good. Theology is not the heedless transmission of a settled and faded truth. Rather it is alive, mediatorial, reinterpretive: it seeks to translate the biblical word about God, man, and the world into our own contemporary concepts and language, to mediate its older thought-forms of another day and another culture to our own day and culture. The goal is to *re*present the biblical word in terms that are intelligent, convincing, and relevant to the life and world in which we actually live. Such are, or should be, the purposes of theology. It is far less important that traditional language be used than that the retranslation express the transcendence or holiness of God's claim on us in Jesus Christ, and His judgment and grace in our lives. Above all, what is necessary is that what is said be intelligible, relevant, and credible—lest all holiness vanish in dogmas that are conventional but ignored. Only then, if it is made a convincing part of

the real world in which we live, can the Word relate itself to our
own existence and transform it.

The sectarian groups from which many of us have come
wanted to free the much-read and continually pondered Scriptures from the unreal and outmoded shell of orthodox interpretations which had erected (so they believed) a barrier between
believing man and the Word of God in Scripture. Today we
consider ourselves in the same situation when we speak of having
"no creed, no theologies, only the Bible," and regard ourselves
as "Bible people" because we have no creedal requirements or
theological instruction in our churches. But exactly the opposite
is in fact the case. Largely because of this antitheological tradition, in these churches the Bible is not mediated to the layman
in terms he can understand and believe; thus he seldom looks at
it. In trying to take it "straight," the layman finds the sacred
Book, with its miracles and strange values, unintelligible and
incredible. When our laymen are *in* culture, theological learning
is the sole medium through which the Bible can speak relevantly
and authoritatively to their minds. We shall today become a
Bible people only if our churches are also centers of theological
teaching and discussion.

Thus if the biblical word is to be an authority in our churches
—if they are to be Bible churches *in* culture—there must be
theological instruction in the church: instruction in the Bible, its
history, and its meanings; instruction in its theological ideas of
God, man, and the cosmos, and in the history of those ideas in
the life of the church; instruction in the relation of those ideas
to our contemporary scientific and philosophical concepts; and
finally, instruction in the ethic of the Bible and its relevance to
our own current problems. Only thus can the intelligent layman
come to realize the authority of the Bible over his own mind
and life—for only thus did each of the clergy, in so far as he
can now read the Bible with comprehension and devotion, come
to understand, appreciate, and live under that authority. If
this seems to mean adult classes and catechetical instruction of
young people in the churches, the inference is correct—it
means exactly that. The role of the minister as *teacher of adults*
and as instructor in Christian ideas and values to every entering
member of the church, is as old as the early catechetical classes

for candidates coming to the church out of the pagan world.[19] It is as old as the assumption that a man or a child must *learn* Christian beliefs, since he comes to them neither by nature nor by birth. The only reason the sects formerly believed they could dispense with this regular instruction was because each member lived in the world of these ideas and immersed himself and his family in the Scriptures through daily readings. Neither activity is characteristic of our laity today. The result is that, unless we teach them in the church, the laity will become progressively more and more ignorant of the beliefs and doctrines as well as of the ethical standards of Christianity.

It is not irrelevant to recall at this point that the favorite goal of every intelligent contemporary B.D. student is to be a teacher first of all. If this is so, then the real field for the pedagogical harvest is neither the college campus nor the seminary, but the local church—where he alone must be almost a one-man seminary. Strangely enough, we are saying that *because*, as the Reformation cried and neo-orthodoxy cried again, the church lives from the Word of God alone—from theology—*therefore* the church in its practical existence can only be saved by religious education! Thus are two ancient enemies reconciled.

Protestantism depends not only on the learned guidance of the preacher, but also on the educated religion of the layman. The Word of God through which Christ rules his church can only come as authority to a congregation that is listening, through preaching, instruction, communal decision, and worship, for that Word in its midst. Thus preaching and teaching are the human media through which the Word enters the church. When it is thus proclaimed, heard, and obeyed, then, as the Reformers said, the church becomes at the same time holy and the true mediating source of God's saving grace.

At the close of this chapter on the church as bearer of the Word of God, it may not be amiss to say something of the vocation of the parish ministry. In our day broad and straight is the

---

[19] "That there was almost no mention of the teaching function of the ministry and its capacity for leadership in a fuller comprehension of the meaning of the faith which the church espouses, would seem to be of some importance." Obenhaus, *op. cit.*, p. 157.

way toward the teaching ministry in college or seminary, and many good students there be who walk that path; but narrow and tortuous is the way to the parish, and few there be that find it. The forces that make the vocation of the local ministry so intensely difficult are of course legion; but two can, I think, be especially singled out: secularism and conservatism.

By secularism I mean the imprisonment of the mind in this world and its affairs: the fundamental sense 'that reality lies here and nowhere else, that all causes are natural or human causes, that all events therefore begin and end here, and all real interests lie solely in this world. This powerful sense of earthly reality and nothing else makes all our words about God, about His judgment, our guilt, and His forgiveness, in fact about any other dimensions and concerns of life, seem unreal even to those who wish to believe. We all feel the shadow of emptiness when we talk religious language in our day to someone who faces despair, or sin, or death. How hard it is therefore for the minister to utter the words which he is there to utter! How easy to talk rather of church clubs, or expanding budgets, enlarged plant, and so on!

By conservatism I mean the imprisonment of the heart in suburbia—or its small-town equivalent. The turns and twists of social and economic history in our land have meant that with few exceptions our churches have, like eager camp followers, plodded along after the rising middle classes. When these latter lived in brownstone fronts, solid churches kept guard at city street corners; when they moved to the suburbs, the churches dutifully followed them thither. Placed so crucially in the wealthy power centers of our land, supported largely by the privileged third, our churches, though they be filled with good people who wish to do good, can only repeat the words of Mary in a faraway voice and with a strange sense of unreality: "He hath showed strength with his arm: he hath scattered the proud in the imagination of their hearts. He hath put down the mighty from their seats, and exalted them of low degree. He hath filled the hungry with good things; and the rich he hath sent empty away" (Luke 1:51-53). When, therefore, the parish minister seeks to *enact* the message of these words, to fill the poor with good things and, when need be, to send the rich (or the white) empty away, inevitably he finds himself isolated, distrusted, and ignored. How much easier to keep the church running smoothly, to increase its missionary giving, and to swell its rolls!

The confluence of these two forces in and on all of us, imprisoning our minds in this world and our hearts in suburbia, makes the task of the minister incredibly difficult. For he must preach a duty and a call which his conservative congregation do not wish to hear, and he must make this claim on their lives in terms of a God and a spiritual existence in which they can barely believe. The religious dimensions of church life: those which deal with the love of God and the love of man, the dimensions pointed to in the first and second Commandments, thus find themselves pushed to the periphery of church life, relegated to small cell groups that study and ponder the Bible, and still smaller contingents that join the brave minister—if he is lucky— in the demonstrations downtown. The larger proportion are immersed in the thousandfold works of the church, activities that concern everything under heaven except these two Commandments. The result has been a discouraged ministry: wishing to preach theology and to lead in moral battles, the typical pastor finds himself the organizer of innumerable but meaningless activities. He longs for academia where he can do both: ponder and teach theology amid an intellectual society, and throw himself without reprisal into social causes. He sees himself locked up and immobilized in the parish, while the real life of theology and of Christian morals goes on in the seminary or the college.

Now what must be said is that this image of the parish as an immobile prison is false—for *this* is the firing line, *this* the frontier, *this* the "marches" of the church! As the army officer in the field was to the desk job in Washington, so is the active minister to his sedentary colleague in the seminary, and the question as to which of them is really immobilized can be by no means simply answered. For as with the field officer, the minister is the one who *does* what at best the theologian may think and plan—and ever since the Incarnation the church has rightly been much more interested in the deed or event than in mere thought. In the most real sense the minister is the one in the church who continues the Incarnation, who recreates continually in history the possibility of Emmanuel, of God with us, and so of the reality of salvation.

The most pressing contemporary theological problem, debated long and arduously in seminary classes and seminars, is: How can we speak meaningfully and relevantly of God in a secular and empirical age? What do God and His will *mean* in the space age, the age of computers and commuters, when the things and values of this life seem so overwhelmingly real and all else so very unreal? How are we to talk of God's rule over our history when Birmingham is so stubborn, Chicago's ghetto so crushing, and Dallas so utterly meaningless? How can we speak to this age of God? So ponder the theologians. But what does the minister *do*, except what the theologians are talking about? Namely, Sunday after Sunday to speak about God to the people of this age? The theologian ponders the very possibility of what the parish minister must accomplish weekly. For unless the Word is present in actuality, the church dies.

We in the seminaries write as best we can about the glory, the judgment, and the love of God. The task of the preacher is far more difficult. It is to make this glory, this judgment, and this love *real* in the midst of a community of men, to bring to bear on the concrete issues of parish life the reality of God's presence through His Word of judgment and of promise. When that Word is so presented, then in the congregation there can be real awe and wonder at His glory, real contrition and repentance before His judgment, and real gratitude and acceptance of for-giveness—and a new life of love becomes possible. Thus is God present in His church, and thus can the church continue as the community within which the Spirit is active in history. In this way, as Catholicism has always rightly insisted, the ministry is a continuation of the Incarnation, a human means through which Emmanuel, God with us, transpires.

Again, in the realm of ethics the problems that concern a seminary scholar run something like this: What should a Chris-tian do in our day? How can we truly love our neighbor in an industrial, suburban, atomic age? These are baffling intellectual problems, like those of religious language, and to them the seminary professor seeks to give inspiring intellectual answers.

In the parish, however, more must be wrestled with than mere ideas and the recalcitrance of difficult answers. The happy teacher in these days of social controversy is protected as in an almost impenetrable castle: his working society is that of a liberal community, and at each drawbridge are administrators trained to keep the wolves outside the walls from snapping at his scholarly shanks. Not so the preacher! He lives and works in the midst of the wolves, that is, in the midst of those immersed in the power conflicts of our society. Through the very people he addresses and seeks to lead, surge the passions, prejudices, irrational hatreds, and virulent defenses of privilege that plague our social order. And if they do not rise against him to remove him when he speaks to them or tries to lead them, still he encounters the molasses-in-January slowness of all privilege when an issue of social justice is raised. His is the intensely difficult task, not of pondering solutions to moral problems, but of enacting them in and through the community of which he is the leader. For a congregation can only become the church in truth when, through hearing the Word, it in some measure itself becomes a community of love and reconciliation, and through that love witnesses to God's love in the society around it. Again the minister is called to incarnate rather than merely discuss the love of God. Because of this far higher calling, his role is correspondingly more dangerous—dangerous to his job, his faith, and his own sense of assurance. For how isolated and lonely he can become! Dedicated to justice in the desert of white exclusiveness, committed to reconciliation in the wastelands of the upper middle class, he is beset by problems and frustrations far greater than those of St. Anthony, and he is far more alone. How lonely is the minister who today goes to jail as a picket, while the elders with and for whom he labors sit on the school boards, the rent-control boards, and the better business boards, defending what he demonstrates against! Here is where the love of God in our age is acted out, not just analyzed in books; here is where lives are tempted and so faithfulness really proven. Again in the true ministry the Incarnation is continued in our midst, in all its humiliation, its loneliness, its despair, and its ultimate victory.

The deepest affirmation of the free-church tradition about the church is that the people, not just the minister, make up the church. It is the congregation, not the ministers' association, that constitutes the People of God. But unless the minister leads, the congregation cannot become a true congregation, the People of

God, a people listening for God's word of judgment, love, and call to obedience, and enacting in their community the love and reconciliation of the Lord's life. In many parts of our land, as we have seen in these pages, a minister is regarded as one called to a special holiness, and often this is a tobaccoless, humorless, fleshless, dry piety that almost removes the blood from his veins and certainly the laughter from any group he approaches. This holiness is a false shadow of the true sanctity to which he is called, and on which the church really does depend: the courage to speak the word of judgment as well as love, the fidelity to bring God's claim to bear on the congregation's life, and the selflessness to incarnate the love of God in his own life as the leader of the congregation. Unless a minister has this courage and faithfulness—both an intellectual honesty and a wily practicality; unless through his forthright words the Word itself can speak, and through his dedicated life be incarnated, there can scarcely be a real congregation. There is no church without him, and little else therefore that matters. He is in his day the servant of the Lord and truly the hope of the world.

5

The Church as the Body of Christ

In our discussion of the first two symbols of the church, I have spoken of the new humanity, the People of God, bound together by the divine spirit of love, harmony, and peace; and of the lordship of Christ, symbol of the church as the community of whom He is the Head, a congregation of people responsibly, repentantly, and faithfully seeking and listening to the Word of God in its midst. But the church is more than this: it is also the communion of the faithful who have fellowship with their Lord. It is, in the third great symbol upon which we shall meditate, the Body of Christ in which the living Spirit of the risen Lord dwells.[1]

We Protestants use often and warmly the word "fellowship." Usually we mean our fellowship one with another, which often refers only to friendliness, but may mean, as we saw, a deeper unity in the Spirit of mutual love, forbearance, and trust. And we also speak of individual fellowship with God, the communion in devotion and in prayer of the individual soul with God in

[1] Rom. 12:4-5; I Cor. 12:12-31; Eph. 1:22-23, 5:22-33; Col. 1:14-18, 24. Cf. the article by F. J. Taylor in A. Richardson, ed., *A Theological Word Book of the Bible* (London: SCM Press, 1950), pp. 35-36.

Christ; our hymns are filled with powerful references to this individual relationship with Christ. The early church, however, was very conscious of a third kind of fellowship which it felt to be the basis of the other two: the fellowship of the congregation, of the church, with the risen Lord in worship: "For where two or three are gathered together in my name, there am I in the midst of them."[2] And for Paul to be "in Christ" meant to be in the worshiping community or congregation where the Spirit of Christ dwells; that is, to be in His Body, the church.[3] Thus for the apostles it was because the risen Lord was in the midst of His community as a living Spirit that the other two types of fellowship were possible, namely, that we could each as individuals have fellowship with him, and that we could have human fellowship in the spirit of love one to another.

All through these chapters I have said that the church was "more" than the individuals who make it up. And now we can say what that "more" is: it is the presence of the risen Lord in the congregation, communicating Himself to us in the Word and having fellowship with us as we meet together in our common worship of Him. The church, then, is not formed merely by the mutual agreement to come together of repentant and regenerate people. It is formed fundamentally by the calling of each one of us by Jesus Christ through his Word, and by His presence in grace and power in the midst of the faithful congregation. The church is the Body of Christ where His Spirit dwells.[4]

[2] Matt. 18:20, 28:20.

[3] Cf. The excellent articles by A. Nygren, A. Fredrichsen, and H. Odeberg in A. Nygren, ed., *This Is the Church* (Philadelphia: Muhlenberg, 1952), esp. pp. 9-12 and 67-72.

[4] "It is in the risen Lord and his spirit that it (the church) is possessed of its existence. The New Testament view of the Church is marked above all by the vivid experience of the activity of the Lord and his Spirit in the congregation, an activity which is prerequisite for the performance of its religious function, for all Christian activity." Fredrichsen, *op. cit.*, p. 16. Or as Nygren puts this in even stronger language: "Christ's body is Christ himself. The Church is Christ, by reason of the fact that since His resurrection he is present with us and meets with us on earth." *Op. cit.*, p. 10. (How close this is to Catholic theory may be seen in the references for Chap. I of this book, n. 1 and 4). And finally F. H. Taylor: "In the earlier epistles, and in Romans and I Corinthians, Christ is conceived as the whole body of which Christians are members in particular; in Ephesians and Colossians the Church is the body and Christ is the head . . . , thus suggesting the absolute dependence of the Church upon Christ for its very

Now for the early church, the way in which the congregation together had fellowship with the risen Lord, the way in which His presence in their midst was realized and inwardly appropriated, was in or through the worship of the community, and especially through its sacraments.[5] In their regular gatherings, centered as they were around both baptism and the Lord's Supper, each individual was brought into immediate communion with Christ, and the vital center of the community was thereby renewed and its common life empowered and sanctified.

In these common acts of worship, then, the earliest congregations continued their fellowship with Christ, and through these acts the Spirit of Christ flowed into the community which was His Body.[6] And yet, as we all know, there is no point where

---

existence, its growth and strength. The fulness which is in the head flows into the body and maintains the order of the body." In A. Richardson, *op. cit.*, p. 35.

[5] As Cyril Richardson puts this: "Furthermore, the Christians were not just a body; they were one body in *Christ*. The word has an upward reference of supreme importance . . . The metaphor is further developed by Paul when he speaks of Christ as the Head of the Church. The underlying concept is the complete dependence of the Christian community upon Christ, who guides, rules and directs it, and to whose control the Church is ever submissive . . . Just as the right of baptism initiated men into the Christian community, so the sacrament of the Lord's Supper was the continuation of the life of Christ in the Church." C. C. Richardson, *The Church Through the Centuries* (New York: Scribner's Sons, 1950), p. 23. "But for the understanding of the cultus in early Christianity, one aspect of the life of the disciples with him is of great importance: the communion between the disciples and Jesus . . . It was just this fellowship that later became central in the early Christian worship. Its inner characteristic was that they knew themselves to be in real fellowship with the risen and present Christ . . . that fellowship with Christ was experienced not merely as something conceived or believed, but as real. Christ was *actually* present when they assembled in his name . . . Their meetings became services of worship, cultic gatherings, because of the presence of the Risen One in the Word, in their prayers offered in his name, and above all in the high point of their coming together, the common meal, and the breaking of bread." Erik Sjöberg, "Church and Cultus in the New Testament," in Nygren, *op. cit.*, pp. 79-81. Let us note how, as these words imply, each of the three major biblical symbols of the church's existence—the People of God in love, the Word of God, and the Body of Christ—points to the presence and activity of Christ in the community. They thus all symbolize His lordship or headship and the community's dependence on that presence for its life.

[6] "This fellowship with Christ is the nerve of the whole practice of

present Protestant life exhibits a greater poverty than in worship and in the sacraments. We perform each of the "ordinances" solemnly, and we speak often of "worshipful experiences." When, however, we ask our laymen why, aside from the pressure of tradition and custom, we perform the sacraments, or what good they are to man or God, few answers are forthcoming; and when we inquire into what the worshipful experiences are, we find little sense of the divine presence, but rather only a kind of contented mood engendered by familiar hymns and procedures.[7] As countless seminary students witness, the deepest reason for the contemporary movement of clergy from the free into the liturgical churches lies in the barrenness of worship in the former and the religious emptiness of their sacramental life. My purpose in this chapter, therefore, is to try to explore how our present serious difficulties with worship and the sacraments have arisen; and, seeing in what ways they were vital and powerful in the New Testament church, to discover if possible how to strengthen them today.

For worship is central to the Christian religious life, as essential as prayer. It is the corporate relationship to God, the community coming consciously into the presence of God together. This is the most direct touch with the holy that humans can have, and thus the heart of religion and of the religious quality of the church. A church may be filled with creative ideas and overflowing with good works, but unless there be a sense of the presence of the holy there, of the presence of God—unless there

---

worship in early Christianity. For that reason it has its center in the sacrament, where that fellowship is experienced with particular definiteness . . . The most notable characteristic of his [Paul's] concept of baptism is his development of the thought about the fellowship with Christ which is established by baptism . . . In baptism the recipient is incorporated with Christ, so that he first dies with him and then arises with him . . . one is in a new creation, because he is in Christ . . . The fellowship with Christ, which began in baptism, one subsequently experienced in the cultus. The thought of the presence of Christ was, as we saw, the most vital fact. And the cultus comes to its high point in the Lord's Supper." *Ibid.*, pp. 85-90.

[7] Cf. the discovery in his survey of the almost complete absence on the part of laymen of concern for or thought about the worship and sacramental life of the church, in Victor Obenhaus, *The Church and Faith in Mid-America* (Philadelphia, Westminster Press, 1963), pp. 136, 158 f.

be a capacity for worship—it is doubtful whether what is there is religion. Worship is not centrally an experience of *ours;* it is meaningless to speak of a "worshipful experience" as if the holy were compounded of a clever arrangement of various kinds of lighting, sober music, proper tones of voice, and the softness or hardness of the pews, all so manipulated as to create a certain experience in us. Such "client-centered" worship does not extend beyond the ceiling of the sanctuary, for here by finite media we seek to take the place of the holy, to create it synthetically. To these efforts to create a worshipful mood the usual congregational response is appropriate: "Preacher, I enjoyed it!" But neither our manipulation nor their enjoyment are categories appropriate to worship. For God, not our own consciousness, is the object of worship; we experience *Him,* not ourselves worshiping. Worship is a response to the presence of God, our reaction to the appearance of the holy. And the point is not that we *feel* something then, though surely reverence, awe, and wonder are normal; but that we relate ourselves creatively to Him, that we respond to His presence in adoration and praise, in confession of sin and thanksgiving for mercies known and received. It is the relation to God, the felt relation to the holy—to the tremendous, majestic, awesome power and goodness of God—that is the core of worship. Thus we bow, thus we adore, thus we surrender ourselves—thus we experience *God.*

When we seek to make intelligible our present situation of dried-up, empty secularity in our worship, one principle is essential for understanding: the holy always appears through definite media or symbols. These media change widely in church history, it is true, and different forms of the church have emphasized different media. But wherever religion is vital, and wherever worship has therefore some reality and meaning, there some definite medium of the holy is to be found around which the church is built, be it the holy sacraments of Catholicism, the sacred Word in the Reformation churches, or the emotional experience of personal salvation in the evangelical churches. One might add that meaningful church architecture is likewise constructed around the central principle of worship, i.e., around the fundamental mediating locus or instrument of the holy—for example, either the altar in Catholicism or the high pulpit in the Reformed churches.[8]

Now, as I have noted, the sectarian and evangelical Christianity from which our modern denominations have largely sprung dispensed with the centrality of outward, objective symbols of the holy in order to free the inward media. Sacramental and liturgical symbols (such as candles, pictures, altars, statues, the cross, and of course the reserved Host on the altar), were taken from the churches, the holiness of objective dogma was rejected, and even the Calvinist sense of the sanctity of holy preaching of the Word from a massive pulpit was compromised. In their place was put the inner experience of the Spirit, or of the Inner Light as with the Quakers, illumining a close fellowship gathered in a bare, conventional room; or, in the nineteenth century, the ecstatic experience of conversion in response to an evangelical witness delivered from a platform in a theaterlike auditorium. Such nonliturgical, nonsacramental, nondoctrinal churches, stripped of all objective, visible symbols, were however in the sects and in their evangelical descendants not at all vacant of experience of the holy, the sense of the presence of the divine. Far from it. In an old Quaker meeting or in a Methodist revival, the holy was present and worship had tremendous power. But the media, though definite and understood, were inward and subjective rather than outward and objective. That is to say, the holy was experienced inwardly, in the inner consciousness—as the Inner Light in Quakerism or the moving

---

[8] There are, of course, several sorts of criteria, esthetic as well as religious, relevant to church architecture. The central *religious* criterion, however, springs from the mode of mediation of the holy in the form of the religion in question. That is, the architecture should express and emphasize that medium within or through which the holy communicates itself to the congregation in worship—e.g., the altar in Catholicism, the high pulpit in Calvinism, or the commonality and equality of worshipers touched by the Spirit in sectarian groups. It is "good" architecture religiously when in this way the form of the building fits—i.e., expresses—the form of worship or of the holy. It is bad architecture when, however "beautiful" or "worshipful" or "like a church" it may be or seem, the form of the building has little relation to the form of worship taking place inside it—as, e.g., when a Methodist, Baptist, or Disciples church has a split chancel which architecturally points to the altar in the middle; but without a "reserved host" to put on it, all that can be set on this table in a focal position is a vase of cut flowers or the morning's collection!

of the Spirit in Methodism—not through objective media such as a sacramental element, an icon, a cross, or even a doctrine or sermon. Because these sectarian congregations lived in continual contact with the divine will, through daily Scripture reading, family prayer, and the separated habits of their lives, even in the simplest, barest rooms their own inner spirits could become, and often were, genuine channels for a sense of the holy.[9]

Our problem is that the social changes in the life of denominational groups have brought about changes as well in the effectiveness and meaningfulness of these subjective forms of worship. Let me give an example: the Quakers have had, as we all know, as vivid and effective a mode of worship as church history has produced, quite without objective symbols, liturgy, reading of the Holy Word, sacraments, preaching, orders of service, or any other observable media. The medium of the holy for them was the Inner Light, the voice of the divine conscience and the divine reason that speaks, as they affirm, in the heart of each believing man. The Quakers thus pushed the sectarian principle of subjectivity, inherited by most of our denominational traditions, to its limit. Some of their current problems may, therefore, illumine to us our own.

When the writer lived in Poughkeepsie, he was often invited (if the "minister" was out of town) to come and address the

---

[9] There seems to be little doubt that subjective emotionalism, as a medium for the holy, flourishes most easily among the less-privileged, where "breeding" and "education" and their resultant "manners" have not yet cramped the dynamic of life's emotions with the straightjacket of formalism. Most examples of corporate emotional religion (Montanism, die Schwärmerei, the Methodists in eighteenth-century England, and the revival churches in our rural districts, white and Negro alike) have occurred among lower-class groups; and further, when they shed their lower-class status the *same* groups quickly shed their emotionalism as well. It is not accurate, however, to associate *subjective* media of the holy with lower-class status, for subjective, or inward, mediation of the holy can take other forms than those of emotional outbursts: for example, contemplative, mystical, or even rational experience of the presence and/or guidance of God. The best illustration of this is, of course, the Quakers, who were by no means solely lower-class at any point in their history, but whose view of the holy, albeit rational and mystical in character, was certainly inward or subjective. Our suggestion here is, then, not so much that the class status of these groups is of sole importance, as that their sociological situation as either a "separated" or a "culturated" group is important in providing the necessary framework for such inward experience of the holy.

local Quaker meeting—requested, that is, to prepare a "sermon" and deliver it at a definite point in the "service."[10] When the layman who extended this invitation was asked why they had so radically changed the form of Quaker worship as to have a paid minister, hymns, order of service, and sermon, he answered: "I was raised a Quaker in a Quaker family, and grew up surrounded by a Quaker community—and the Inner Light spoke to all of us at the meetings we had together. But when we moved here to Poughkeepsie, and I began to sell stocks and bonds, all I could think of in that silence was the Dow-Jones stock averages —and so we wanted to have people who didn't think only of the market all week long to talk to us about religion." One could put his—and our—problem this way: when the whole of a man's life is suffused with contact with the divine, in daily Bible reading, the requirements of a strict communal ethic, and constant habits of prayer, then through the total character of his life his subjectivity is saturated with the dimension of the holy, and he can go into a bare room, sit in silence, and religious and ethical wisdom wells up inside him. But the man whose daily life is immersed in secular, cultural, and business affairs, who seldom reads the Bible, and whose life of personal prayer is at best feeble, erratic, and unsure—when *he* goes to that bare room, divested of all religious symbols and all objective media for the holy, there is no holy *anywhere* for him to experience, and his mind is filled, and naturally so, with the stuff of his life, the Dow-Jones stock averages.

Here, in a nutshell, is the present Protestant problem of worship. The social conditions for the removal of objective symbols or media of the holy are now gone. The divine qualifies neither the communal nor the family life of our people during the week. The Bible has become a strange and little-used book;

[10] It should be said plainly that I do not mean by this example to imply that the situation of this Quaker group, which I recall with great appreciation, is typical of all Quaker meetings or even a majority, though it becomes more typical as one moves westward away from the East. I know that many meetings have been able to withstand the pressures of culture against inward religion and maintain their tradition intact even in the modern world. This case merely served to illumine in an amazingly clear way the dynamic factors at work in *all* sectarian groups when they have joined the culture and have subsequently experienced an impoverishment of their peculiarly subjective forms of worship.

the family religion of Scripture readings and prayers has abdicated in favor of what the church can provide on Sunday; and the standards, values, and concepts of ordinary lay life are completely derived from secular society. Thus the average churchgoer comes into church out of a life, not saturated with the holy, but quite devoid of all but secular content in ideas, experiences, and values. Consequently his inner consciousness is worldly in the extreme; the true world to him is the causal and human world around him, in which the dimension of the holy is unknown. How can he, out of this secular inwardness, have an experience of God, of worship, from his own subjectivity, from himself alone—how can he worship unless there are objective media for the holy? The sectarian layman is *in* the world now; and, as in each facet of the church's life, this new social situation makes a vast difference. It means that in our day worship can occur only where some powerful symbolic mediation of the holy takes place.[11]

As we have noted further, those media which did communicate the holy in traditional American Protestant church life have been weakened. The older Calvinist sense that the Bible, in a place of honor on the high pulpit, read and expounded, was the vehicle of the holy in worship—and that we could thus allow all other symbols to vanish from the church—is not avail-

[11] While the renewed interest in the Episcopal Church has many causes, and is of course more a clerical than a lay phenomenon, nevertheless when the non-Episcopalian, lay or cleric, is asked the reasons for this interest, the answer is almost invariably something like this: "They seem to have more of a real sense of worship," "There seems to be more real *religion* in their services," "I feel the presence of God when I go to church there"; and so on. These replies clearly indicate that at present the worshiper has more of an *experience* of the holy in churches which have objective media of the holy—i.e., liturgical forms and symbols, and above all, meaningful sacraments—than in those which, having forsaken objective media in order to emphasize inner experience, now find themselves devoid of the very experiences they once fostered. Another irony in this connection appeared to the author when a ministerial student, explaining why he was changing to the Episcopalian clergy from the Methodist, said: "I want my ministry to be a religious and not a secular vocation. And I mean by that, one connected with inwardness, the holy, and the things of God, and not merely with the various activities, functions, and programs of the visible church." The irony is that very much the same reasons would have been put forward by a serious young eighteenth-century minister to explain why he was leaving the Church of England to join those who called themselves Methodists.

able to us. For most of us the Bible is as much a human and fallible document as it is the oracle of God; and anyway, whatever the laity's theology of Scripture, the familiarity with its message is far less than it was a hundred years ago.

More characteristic probably as the vehicle of the holy in the Protestant churches of America was a vivid emotional experience, in response to someone's witness to the working of the Holy Spirit. In most of the evangelical churches of nineteenth-century America the sermon was less a declaration of the Word of God than a witness to the Spirit's work in one's own life and a call to similar holy experiences in the congregation. But this form of worship has also been weakened by social change. The people who could experience such emotional upheavals and revivals were on the whole themselves rural and small-town folk whose habits of life were generally so little formalized that strong and sudden expressions of emotion not only came easily to them, but also provided their most vivid contact with reality. Just as they could snap their galluses at town meeting, hit the cuspidor in the kitchen at fifteen paces, put their feet on the stove in the country store, and take off their collars except when they went to church or the city, so could they with appropriateness be violently moved by religion, experience a sudden change of life, and unashamedly shout "Amen!" in church. To such rural people a formalized, esthetically elegant liturgical religious service was as unnatural as it was unconnected with their own tastes; in no sense could it be for them a vehicle of the holy—mostly because nothing in their lives had this sort of formal character.

Between their rural folk existence and that of their present-day descendents, however, a great gulf is fixed, dug out by the social changes in these groups. For their grandchildren have now moved to the suburbs, been educated at college, and listen to Bach (or at least Lombardo) instead of to country music. They sit as politely and quietly in church as in their favorite restaurants or at a symphony, and an "Amen, Brother!" from the next pew would make them as uncomfortable and nervous as a spittoon in their living room. Most of our urban and suburban people, in moving upward in culture, have become more formalized in their esthetic and religious tastes. The formality that would have seemed a hypocritical sham to their rural grandfathers is to them the "nice" way to do things. And the kind of service in which for their elders there would have been real—because emotional—religion has become hopelessly countrified and primitive to them. Countless students returning to their home-town churches after a year of college or seminary, in which their esthetic tastes and modes of life have become more formalized and structured, are surprised and deeply offended at how rustic and "corny" the services they used to love have suddenly become. Ironically, a vivid emotional experience of conversion is as unavailable to the modern well-heeled suburban Methodist as it was to the aristocratic Church of Englander in the eighteenth century, who looked down on "those emotional people called Methodists."

Thus have the objective media of the infallible Bible and a vivid emotional experience lost their symbolic power to modern educated suburban congregations. In some of them the folksyness remains as a pathetic nostalgia for bygone days of conversions and revivals—pathetic because no such emotional revelations of the holy now course through the pews, however informal the hymn-singing and the lingo may be. In most denominations, however, rural informality has given way to an educated middle-class formality, without any corresponding vehicle of the holy to give substance to worship. Thus in place of the evangelical experience have appeared prayers as essays in introspection, the pulpit as a lecture platform, sacred music as a kind of amateur concert, the communion table as an attractive stand for flowers and candles and a handy place for the offertory plates; while in the pews are people listening to an inspirational address that calls them to renewed activity and revitalized giving in the church—people waiting for the fellowship coffee hour when they will see their friends. This sounds grim, but empirical studies show over and over that these are in fact the elements remembered and meaningful in the present-day religious pattern.

The results of this change are everywhere evident. Revivals are held in all the free churches of the South and into the rural Midwest, but usually only the most faithful members attend, and no vivid experiences occur or are expected. The old gospel hymns are sung, but the experiences they relate—experiences of being "sunk in sin" and "rescued by Jesus"—are not known to the smooth suburban layman with his executive's self-control. As orthodox dogmas have become signs of church loyalty and not symbols of the truth, so the experiences related in the gospel hymns are for most laymen nostalgic recollections of their parents' religion, not their own. And this nostalgia is poignantly expressed in the remark repeatedly heard in our churches: "That was *real* religion"—real, but at present not experienced by those who try to profess it.[12]

Because the effectiveness of the two traditional evangelical media of the holy, the sacred biblical Word and the presence of the Spirit, is rapidly disappearing, little sense of it remains in our worship. Moral and social respectability and the personal fellowship of the church have become the important things. Over and over one hears in the South, "Come to our church—it is friendly and we have wonderful fellowship," or "We have such a fine and growing Sunday school." But *not*, "You will hear

[12] Nostalgia is, I believe, the most dangerous cancer in the life of present Southern religion. By nostalgia I mean the effort to hold on to an older, parental (and even grandparental) form of religion, not because it has direct and relevant meaning to present existence, but because it symbolizes a way of life and of viewing life which, looked back on, seems serene, secure, meaningful, and good. It is the memory of mother singing those gospel hymns that is meaningful to men when they sing them, *not* the message of the hymn as heard by them now. It is the conviction that there was "real religion" in those days—and that they have somehow lost it—that drives them to assert these forms of strict biblical belief and folksy patterns of worship, though all are modern men in everything else they believe and not at all "folksy" in their other social activities and relations in suburbia. I have called such religion nostalgic because the tie that binds the worshiper to it is not his own personal belief and commitment to a present God, but a sentimental hankering for the yesteryear which this religion symbolizes. The particular message about God, sin, and salvation for which this form of religion stands is neither experienced nor really believed in at all, for it seems to modern industrial and suburban men and women quite unreal. On the contrary, the emotional tone that characterizes such religion is one of longing and not belief; and what is longed for is not so much a contemporary walk with Jesus as to recapture aspects of the old life of which the religion reminds us.

Certainly many aspects of that now departed style of life represented by "old-time religion" may well be acutely missed in our anxious, impersonal, urban age. For that older style of life incorporated all the values of homey small-town America, with its close personal relations, its secure moral standards, and its ultimate certainties about the nature of things. This entire complex of relationships, standards, and certainties has been rudely shattered by the modern technological and commercial era, with its per-

there the Word of God, or meet the Spirit." And if a controversial sermon is preached, folks are polite, but amazed and bewildered. The presence of the holy, and so all real transcendence, has gone, and with it, in the now familiar pattern, has gone also all relevance.

My central thesis has been that social change in the lives of Protestant people has brought about important changes in the religious quality of Protestant church life. The elements of the holy in historic Protestantism have by these changes been shorn of their holiness; the ethical life of Protestantism has become acclimatized to the standards of town and suburb; the ideas and beliefs of our churches are confused, dim, and empty, leaving a residue of vagueness that spells conformity to culture; and now, as we have seen, the earlier emphasis of denominational worship on inner experience has meant, in a secularly conditioned congregation, that the holy has quite vanished from our sanctu-

---

sonal uprootedness and loneliness, its doubt about the reality of all religious affirmations, its new anxieties about the future, and its less restricted but potentially meaningless life of the suburbs. But the wealthy Baptist businessman, comfortable in his Hart, Shaffner and Marx suit and his new Lincoln, who expresses his longing for the small-town past through gospel hymns, revivals, fundamentalist slogans, and folksy worship services, does not really wish or intend to *live* in that rural, bygone age. It does not represent *his* religion, his ultimate commitment, for he is far too attached to the modern world in which he lives and works—to its opportunities, its freedoms, its gadgets, and its values—to relinquish it for the small town he left behind years ago. He only misses certain "spiritual" things about that past life which his present commercial existence seems to lack, and that emptiness of values and beliefs is partially filled by this occasional backward journey in time through his Sunday church life. Since this religion symbolizes for him only a vanished past when other people (not he) believed in God, it is really not his religion but theirs. What is communicated to him by it is only the memory of their religion, not the presence of God. It has, therefore, neither judging nor saving power for him. Further, it will itself die out when he passes on and the memory of that past generation dies. The small-town folksy religion will in a few years not even be an object of nostalgia. The current crop of young people have been brought up in the modern suburbs, in the atmosphere of high-school science, country club social life, and fraternity moral codes, and know nothing at first hand of "old-time religion." Such children of the suburbs will not be able to recall in their adult years, as their parents now do, that "Daddy had this kind of religion"—for our modern suburban daddies do not. All they will be able to say is that "Daddy used to like to sing those old songs," and at that point the accidental connection of gospel religion

aries. In each case I have suggested that the task of contemporary Protestantism, after it has taken a realistic look at this situation, is to rediscover the separated elements that can mediate the holy to the life of man, and I have suggested doing this through a re-examination of the classic symbols of the church's life. In the area of worship this means that Word and Sacrament, as the objective means of grace given to the church, must replace our current weak concentration on subjective experiences of worship if the holy is again to appear in our churches. My fourth chapter was devoted to the problem of the Word and its relation to the modern congregation, and in these final remarks I have turned to the sacraments. What can they mean to a modern congregation, and how may they become living media for the holy in the life of the church?

Let us begin with some thoughts on the sacraments as a whole, and then illustrate them specifically in terms of the Lord's Supper, which has always been a central part of the worship of the Christian church. In the sacraments we find ourselves in the world of symbols: that is, media through which Christ comes to us in faith. Now some of us tend to think of a symbol as if it were merely a sign: a somewhat casually chosen substitute that stands for something else and so reminds us of it when we see it. Thus it is typically felt that the wine (or grape juice) and the bread are reminders of Jesus, and so, in the Lord's Supper, we are merely to think again and anew of Him and what He taught. Symbols, however, are more powerful than this: the power and meaning of what they stand for, the reality they are to remind us of, is not so far away—as if Calvary were still on a hill long ago. Rather, that power and meaning and reality seem to dwell

---

with a natural nostalgia for remembered childhood scenes will have vanished. Because of the present widespread character of this longing for the bygone small-town South, "old-time religion" is at present very popular among the newly mobile and rootless middle classes; correspondingly, the churches (especially the Baptist) that regard it as their mission to guard it continue to grow in numbers. One cannot but suspect, however, that this rate of growth will soon slacken and ultimately die off unless the religion of these churches is made relevant to the thought, the behavior, the emotions, and the social habits of the present-day world.

within them, so that they become for us media for communicating, for presenting, making really present here and now the reality they symbolize.

In our secular experience we are familiar with many symbols of this sort: conceptual ones that create, maintain, and thus make immediately present the spirit or ideology of the community in which we live. Examples in a democratic community are "equal justice," "freedom," "liberty," "the equality of men," "natural rights," and so on. Such symbolic words or phrases have no definite, objective referent that anyone can point to, as does a sign. Their relation to their referents is at once more immediate and more mysterious. For out of these word-symbols arises in a real sense our American community, in so far as they express and present, recreate and make real, the ethos that makes us a democratic community.[13] Symbols are, therefore, foundation stones for the spiritual reality of a community, communicating to every part of it, in space and through time, the spiritual life that creates and recreates it. The great theological symbols that

---

[13] The elusiveness of the referent for the democratic-political symbol "the equality of man" is well known. To what does this symbol refer? To a physical or anthropological equality, to an equality of mental powers, an equality of some sort of "value," or equality in the sight of God? Probably other possibilities equally elusive could be mentioned. Many positivistically inclined friends have pointed out to the writer the impossibility of locating by research or by expedition the referents of such political symbols—but the same friends are more often than not to be found standing up for the rights of minority groups at great personal cost, and appealing in such existential situations, when they forget themselves, to symbols as indefinite as "the rights of men," "the equality of the races," "academic freedom," and so on. This author believes that ultimately an ontological referent for these symbols can be found, a referent that can be expressed most fully in terms of the Christian doctrine of man as the creature and the adopted son of God. But as the history of democracy and the ranks of liberalism show, the symbolic power of these phrases has been much wider than has belief in this theological-philosophical interpretation of their actual referent. For many men have risked their substance for these symbols who knew nothing of an ultimate equality before God. Thus the power of such a symbol is not dependent upon a clear understanding of its referent; rather its power lies in the fact that it expresses and communicates the intangible reality of a democratic spirit, a spirit that lives (if it lives at all) in the convictions and so in the behavior patterns of the members of any community that can be called democratic. Symbols thus point to, express, communicate, and so ultimately realize what they symbolize: the spiritual reality of the community to which they provide form and direction.

make up what the Reformers called "the Word of God" functioned in much the same way in the community of the church—symbols about God and what He has done: creation, incarnation, atonement, and resurrection. These are not doctrines so much as conceptual symbols around which doctrines cluster, whose meaning for each generation doctrines seek to express. Much as a democratic or Communist philosophy is *about* the symbols of a democratic or a Communist community, so a Christian theology is *about* the symbols of the Christian community. And correspondingly the preaching of the Word—the other central element of Protestant worship—is the communication of the relevance and meaning of these verbal symbols to the everyday life and actual existence of the congregation.

Now, strange as it is to our rational and modern ears, words are not the only symbolic media of spiritual reality or communication. Words can express friendship and love, but (though intellectuals hesitate to believe it) a handclasp or an embrace communicates and expresses, and therefore makes real, that friendship or that love far more deeply.[14] If this were not so, we could communicate satisfactorily with our wives and sweethearts over the phone; and everyone knows how untrue that is! ! Thus in all communities and all human relations there are material as well as verbal symbols: physical acts and objects, ceremonies and sacraments, that communicate, express, and make real the common life. In much the same way an academic community is preserved and strengthened not only by such verbal symbols as "academic freedom," "scientific honesty," and "scholarly objectivity," but also by its liturgical ceremonies of oral examination, graduation, and convocation, and its symbolic par-

[14] Calvin gives this same example in explaining the relation of spiritual word to material symbol, be the latter a thing or an act: "What is the contact of one man's right hand with that of another, since hands are not infrequently joined in hostility? But when words of friendship and compact have preceded, the obligations of covenants are confirmed by such signs, notwithstanding they have been previously conceived, proposed and determined in words. Sacraments, therefore, are exercises, which increase and strengthen our faith in the Word of God; and because we are corporeal, they are exhibited under corporeal symbols, to instruct us according to our dull capacities, and to lead us by the hand as so many young children." John Calvin, *Institutes of the Christian Religion*, trans. by J. Allen, Bk. IV, Chap. XIV, sec. VI (Philadelphia: Presbyterian Board of Christian Education, 1936), Vol. II, p. 559.

aphernalia of degrees, diplomas, gowns, hats, batons, and seals.

Material symbols worry us, despite our continual repudiation of the "shallowness of rationalism." We tend to think either that what we expect them to communicate is also material (in which case we now call such thinking "magical") or that, if it is spiritual, then words can do it better. Thus material symbols are apt to seem to us either superstitious or silly; in neither case are they the centers of Christian worship and life that they have always been. Let us recall, however, what both the great Reformers said about the sacraments. Baptism in water and the Eucharist with its bread and wine are sacraments which communicate to faith the same word of promise and of love as do Scripture and preaching.[15] Receiving them in faith, we receive the same gospel of Jesus Christ as is preached and heard from the pulpit. Thus, as supplementary media of the gospel, they are aids and fortifiers of our faith—confirmations and seals of it—for they make present and real what is talked about in the sermon. The writer will never forget a remark of Reinhold Niebuhr shortly after his stroke. He said that at Easter, when we all ask the anxious questions about eternal life, he would rather

[15] "For God does not deal, nor has He ever dealt, with man otherwise than through a word of promise . . . again, we cannot deal with God otherwise than through faith in the word of His promise. . . . But while the mass is the word of Christ, it is also true that God is wont to add to wellnigh every promise of His a certain sign as a mark or memorial of His promise, so that we may thereby the more faithfully hold to His promise and be the more forcibly admonished by it. . . . We learn from this that in every promise of God two things are presented to us—the word and the sign—so that we are to understand the word to be the testament, but the sign to be the sacrament. Thus in the mass the word of Christ is the testament, and the bread and wine are the sacrament." Martin Luther, "The Babylonian Captivity of the Church," *Works of Martin Luther*, Vol. II, (Philadelphia: Muhlenberg, 1943), pp. 201-203. For further discussions of the promise, i.e., the word of the gospel contained in each sacrament, see *ibid.*, pp. 220-221 for baptism, and for the Eucharist, pp. 197-199, 203-204.

And this from Calvin: ". . . we see that there is never any sacrament without an antecedent promise of God, to which it is subjoined as an appendix, in order to confirm and seal the promise itself, and to certify and ratify it to us; which means God foresees to be necessary, in the first place on account of our ignorance and dullness, and in the next place on account of our weakness; and yet, strictly speaking, not so much for the confirmation of his sacred word, as for our establishment in the faith of it." *Op. cit.*, Bk. IV, Chap. XIV, sec. III, Vol. II, p. 556. And again: "For seeing we are so foolish, that we cannot receive him with true confidence

receive the gospel of God's eternal love through the Eucharist than hear some theologian or preacher like himself theorize about it. There is, said he, a directness and a reality in the sacramental symbols of the Word that our own spoken words do not have.

The sacraments, therefore, and especially the Lord's Supper, communicate to us the same Word and gospel as do our reading and speaking. They are, so to speak, the enacted gospel. The reality that is communicated is not a physical reality—a "medicine of immortality" or divine power.[16] What is communicated and so made real is the Word of God; the Sacrament is, as Calvin puts it, "a fleshly mirror of spiritual blessings."[17] What it symbolizes and so makes present is the judgment and the loving mercy of God, and when these come to each one of us as we partake of the Supper in faith, Christ is really present to us, and present in the most direct and real manner possible. When, therefore, these symbols are received in faith—when, that is, the judgment and love of Christ are received through them in real inner repentance and trust, they are neither mere material objects communicating a material medicine, nor merely signs for intellectual reminder. Rather, they present Jesus Christ to our faith, who is to us the Word of God's judgment on our sins

---

of heart, when he is presented by simple teaching and preaching, the Father, of his mercy, not at all disdaining to condescend in this matter to our infirmity, has desired to attach to his word a visible sign, by which he represents the substance of his promises, to confirm and fortify us, and to deliver us from all doubt and uncertainty." "Treatise on the Lord's Supper," I, found in *Calvin: Theological Treatises*, J. K. S. Reid, ed., Library of Christian Classics, Vol. XXII (Philadelphia: Westminster Press, 1954), p. 144.

[16] An expressive but unfortunately materialistic phrase of Ignatius of Antioch (d. 117) in his letter to the Ephesians: "At these meetings you should heed the bishop and presbytery attentively, and break one loaf, which is the medicine of immortality, and the antidote which wards off death but yields continuous life in union with Jesus Christ." "Letter . . . to the Ephesians," sec. 20, *Early Christian Fathers*, C. C. Richardson, ed., Library of Christian Classics, Vol. I (Philadelphia: Westminster Press, 1953), p. 93.

[17] Calvin, *Institutes*, Bk. IV, Chap. XIV, sec. III, *op. cit.*, Vol. II, p. 557, and the following: "Now our heavenly Father . . . gives us the Supper as a mirror in which we contemplate our Lord Jesus Christ crucified to abolish our faults and offenses, and raised to deliver us from corruption and death, and restoring us to a heavenly immortality." "Treatise on the Lord's Supper," II, *Calvin: Theological Treatises*, p. 145.

and of God's mercy and love that will accept us, being sinful, and refashion us, here and in eternity. And when that Word is received inwardly, then the judgment and love of God are immediately present, unqualifiedly real, and effectively active. Instead of implying the unreality or absence of that to which it refers, a symbol *communicates* the reality it symbolizes, when in a community it is received and inwardly participated in. And so it is that through these symbols of Word and Sacrament our Lord is really present in His church.

All well and good, we may say. We need enacted, material symbols in our religious life as well as conceptual ones—granted. But why these particular ones? Can we not fashion others that communicate the gospel to us more clearly—possibly a churchly pageant or some symbolic clerical rite? Why these elements; why washing in water, and why a meal? Why eating? These are more than esoteric questions; they are questions that lie hidden in the minds of us all, lay and clerical, as we approach the Lord's Supper. Isn't it, after all, a bit foolish or "tribal" to eat a dab of bread and drink a few drops of liquid in order to make contact with God in the Christian church? We may note that though as theologically minded Christians we speak often of our distaste for a dualism of mind and body, and of our devotion to historical particularity and uniqueness, yet when we confront these particular symbols and take part in this particular rite, with its physical media and radically historical and so very particular origin, we feel foolish—and know ourselves to be "Greeks" at heart.

The early Fathers were much interested in this question, and wrote often on the symbolic power of bread and wine. Bread and wine (but hardly grape juice, we might ruefully note!) are, they said, the staff of life, the realities by which we exist, which therefore express our absolute dependence on God's power and goodness, and in turn become in us, by the divine miracle of life itself, our own body and blood. As the bread and wine in our ordinary meals nourish our bodies to earthly life, so through them in the heavenly Supper God nourishes our souls and our being to eternal life.[18] Consequently, Christ is our

[18] "And just as a cutting from the vine planted in the ground fructifies in its season, or as a corn of wheat falling into the earth and becoming de-

heavenly bread, and His shed blood our heavenly, or eschatological, wine. In Him and so through His body and blood, we live
eternally as in nature we now live temporally, these two gifts
of natural and then eternal life being the two great miracles of
God's goodness to us. In this sense bread and wine are numinous
entities themselves—sources, and so symbols, of the deep and
even irrational mystery of natural life itself—as are our own
bodies and our blood. Their symbolic power for the divine gift
of eternal life is therefore immense.

As both the early Fathers and the Reformers realized, however,
the historical symbolism of the Eucharist is far more powerful
than the natural.[19] For, as our Lord Himself said, the bread and
the wine refer to the great historical events among which the
first supper was itself enacted.[20] They are symbols primarily
for those acts in which Jesus accomplished our salvation—that
is, for His death and resurrection, in which He became (to revert
to the patristic phrase) our heavenly bread and the wine of
eternal life. Thus in our religion do historical symbols give
meaning to the natural. For in the breaking of the bread (His

---

composed, rises with manifold increase by the Spirit of God, who contains
all things, and then, through the wisdom of God, serves for the use of
man, and having received the Word of God, becomes the Eucharist, which
is the body and blood of Christ; so also our bodies, being nourished by it,
and deposited in the earth, and suffering decomposition there, shall rise at
their appointed time, the Word of God granting their resurrection to the
glory of God, even the Father, who freely gives to this mortal immortality,
and to this corruptible incorruption . . ." Irenaeus, *Against Heresies*, Bk.
V, Chap. II, sec. 3, *The Ante-Nicene Fathers*, Vol. I, (Grand Rapids,
Mich.: Eerdmans, 1950), p. 528.

[19] The close relation of the Lord's Supper to the passion, death, and
resurrection of Jesus has of course always been central to its meaning and
power, as not only the New Testament itself, but the following from
church history make clear: "They hold aloof from the Eucharist and
from services of prayer, because they refuse to admit that the Eucharist is
the flesh of our Savior Jesus Christ, which suffered for our sins and which,
in His goodness, the Father raised [from the dead]." Ignatius, "To the
Smyrnaeans," C. C. Richardson, *op. cit.*, p. 115. In letter 62, Cyprian continually refers to the identity of the sacrifice of Christ on Calvary and the
present action of the Eucharist by and for the people: e.g., ". . . because
just as the drinking of wine cannot be attained unless the bunch of grapes
be first trodden and pressed, so neither could we drink the blood of
Christ unless Christ had first been trampled upon and pressed, and had
first drunk the cup of which He should also give believers to drink."
Cyprian, "Epistle 62," sec. 7, *The Ante-Nicene Fathers, op. cit.*, Vol. V, p.

body) and the pouring forth of the wine (His blood), we re-enact His death for us on the cross. Through that death He brought to us at once the judgment and the loving mercy of God. In that judgment and mercy we are saved and made whole; for we are given faith in God's mercy now, and in prospect we are given the hope of love for Him and for each other. In that faithful relation to the eternal God we are also given hope for eternal life with Him. Faith, hope, and love are thus the vast gifts of Jesus Christ in His life, death, and resurrection for us—the gifts of His broken and now healed body, and of His shed and now living blood, whose symbols for us *now* are the bread and the wine. Thus the Lord's Supper means centrally for our faith not only His fellowship with the disciples in a meal long ago, but the deeper, eternal fellowship in which He takes upon Himself our sin, our death, and even the judgment of God on us. By that fellowship He establishes us in the relation to God which He has Himself, in which we were created, and in which alone we are saved.[21] To receive this message in faith through the bread and the wine is to receive the gospel and to be really present with Christ.

---

360. And even more clearly: "For if Jesus Christ, our Lord and God, is Himself the chief priest of God the Father, and has first offered Himself a sacrifice to the Father, and has commanded this to be done in commemoration of Himself . . . he [the priest] then offers a true and full sacrifice in the Church to God the Father, when he proceeds to offer it according to what he sees Christ Himself to have offered." *Ibid.*, sec. 14, p. 362.

The relation, however, is even more direct in Luther, not here so much as a *repetition* of the sacrifice of Christ, but as a *sign of the promise* involved in the sacrifice in Christ: "The mass, according to its substance, is, therefore, nothing else than the aforesaid words of Christ—'Take and eat'; as if He said: 'Behold, O sinful man and condemned, out of pure and unmerited love wherewith I love thee, and by the will of the Father of all mercies, I promise thee in these words . . . the forgiveness of all thy sins and life everlasting. And, that thou mayest be most certainly assured of this my irrevocable promise, I give my body and shed my blood, thus by my very death confirming this promise, and leaving thee my body and blood as a sign and memorial of this same promise.'" "The Babylonian Captivity of the Church," *Works* (Muhlenberg ed.), Vol. II, p. 199.

[20] Matt. 26:26-29; Mark 14:22-25; Luke 22:14-20; I Cor. 11:23-26.

[21] This deepest fellowship with Jesus through His death, a fellowship of sonship and communion with God, is perhaps most clearly expressed in Heb. 10:12-22. It is, however, also perhaps the central theme of all of Paul's words on salvation (cf. Rom. 5 and 8). This identification with Christ, moreover, in and through His atonement, in which He takes our

Church tradition has always added that we take this one loaf *together*, and that therefore the Supper symbolizes the unity of the fellowship of the church, of our common bonds of love and brotherhood one to another in the worship of Christ.[22] This, one might remark, is the *optimistic* interpretation of this reference to the congregation. A broken body and shed blood point, unfortunately, not only to the Lord's act on Calvary. They point also to us, to our own broken life and fellowship in the church which is His body. There is a terrible irony in our symbolic breaking of this body and pouring out of this wine week after week in the church—symbols as they are of our terrible and costly divisions in the Body of Christ: of churches, races, and nations—and of the blood, fleshly and spiritual, that we shed moment by moment in history in our communities. Here in our continual breaking of His body, the church, and in our shedding of His blood, is the real repetition of the sacrifice of Christ—here is the Mass! Thus these symbols of broken bread and poured wine point not only to man's general need and to Christ's death. They point as well to *our* very present sin and very immediate need. When in faith we know this here and now, we know here and now the judgment of God *on us*—and the Risen One has entered His church and become its Lord in truth. Here He stands among *us*. When we know this judgment on ourselves and our life, we

---

place in sin and we His in righteousness, is the basic motif of Reformation views of the meaning of the atonement. For it is through this identification with us, this transference of what is ours to Him and what is His to us, that Jesus becomes the *Christus pro nobis*, the saving Christ for us, by whom we are justified despite our sin and so through whom we are received into sonship before God. Cf. Luther "Commentary on Galatians," esp. Gal. 3:13 and 4:4 ff. (in the Revell, 1953 edition, pp. 268-82, 353-59), and Calvin, *Institutes*, Bk. II, Chaps. XV and XVI, *op. cit.*, Vol. I.

[22] Cf. the following from Cyprian: "For when the Lord calls bread, which is combined by the union of many grains, His body, He indicates our people whom He bore as being united; and when He calls the wine, which is pressed from many grapes and clusters and collected together, His blood, He also signifies our flock linked together by the mingling of a united multitude." Cyprian, "Epistle 75," sec. 6, *The Ante-Nicene Fathers, op. cit.*, Vol. V, p. 398. This has, incidentally, also been a main theme of the sectarian movement: breaking the bread *together* and taking the cup *together* symbolize the unity in love of the brethren in the church community, cf. B. Hübmaier, "A Form for the Celebration of the Lord's Supper," in H. E. Fosdick, *Great Voices of the Reformation* (New York: Random House, 1952), pp. 311-15.

can know His real presence as healing grace as well. For as He came to His broken and fleeing band of disciples after His death and resurrection, so He comes to us now who, too, have broken His body, bringing us the new life of God's love and forgiveness, and at the end the new life of eternity.

The presence of the Lord in His congregation, as judgment on our sin and as healing love for our wounds, is then the sole source of the power and the reality of these symbols, the sole ground of their value and their permanence among us. Without Him, they, as we, are nothing. Without His immediate judgment—now—on our life, and His wondrous grace, they have only an old historical episode to remind us of, and the mysterious powers of nature to represent to us. It is cheering, when He is so necessary for their efficacy, to remember that we did not choose these symbols. He chose them, and used them, in the best-attested records of the gospel stories. And in using them with His disciples He promised that this bread was to be His body, and this wine the new covenant in His blood. They are not our signs of Him. They are His chosen symbols of His own promise to be in our midst when we take them in repentance, in faith, and in love.

And so we discover again the common answer to our problem in each of its facets. There *is* a transcendent element in the church, namely, the means of grace which God has given in Word and Sacrament, and around these alone can the church be built. The rediscovery of this has been the central motif of the new theology in relation to the church, and the search for this transcendent holy is the central characteristic of each serious seminary student's personal quest. Often he looks at his liberal social-gospel predecessors with disdain as "secular" or, even worse, "immanent." But let us recall that orthodoxy can lose the transcendent as quickly as can liberalism, and that without relevance to our total secular life, both personal and social, the transcendent Word and the holy Sacrament hang there as Sunday appendages of little use to God or man. Only when they are relevant to our own life, its sins, and its needs do Word and Sacrament themselves become media of the holy, and only then is the church a holy people.

When the Word is heard in the congregation in real repentance and in faith—when the sacraments become the medium of the presence of that Word of Christ to each of us in his own immediate situation—then the church can be the new People of God, related to Him in confession and trust, and so related to one another and to their social environment in love and service. Only thus, through the presence of the transcendent, holy God in His congregation and not through any efforts of our own to enlarge our plants, attract more members, or gain more influence, can the church perform its task. For only God is holy, and only He can work wonders through His instrument, the church.

6

Theological Epilogue: Language and the Church

These chapters have been full of words about the church—thousands of them. In our day of concern with types of language, therefore, it may be well to address some final remarks, at least to theological colleagues, about the kinds of language I have sought to use and why I have used some types rather than others —for there have been some rather strange omissions. In this short space I shall by no means exhaust the semantic problems involved in theological discourse; but I may be able to give some justification and explanation of the method in this book.

As any one familiar with the subject will recognize, if he has not done so already, there is a vast confusion in our contemporary language about the church. Its main characteristic seems to be unrelatedness or disjointedness: the church when we speak of it in contemporary ecumenical theology seems to have absolutely nothing to do with the church as we attend it on Sunday or work in it on week nights. For example, if the church is defined thus: "The church is the congregation of faithful people whose sole Lord is Jesus Christ, who listen for the Word of God, and whose hearts are warmed and their minds illumined by the Holy Spirit, and so where agape provides the bond of unity"—how are we to relate *this* church with the middle-class church on the corner of Twelfth and Union? Again, the official descriptions of any one of our denominational communions seem to bear no resemblance at all to the institutions in which we worship and work. For example, most Southern Baptists are accustomed by now to working politically within a gigantic centralized, national operation, seeking more and more members, recognizing as its supreme value the expansion, stability, and unity of this national organization, and granting to its various organs of power immense authority over local congregations and individuals. What is an observant member to think when he hears the official description of his church as a group of "autonomous, convenanted congregations of regenerate, adult and biblically loyal Christians, who have personally experienced salvation, who recognize no spiritual authority but their Bibles, and who are concerned only with the salvation of souls"? In other words, there seem to be different realities, all called "church," that exist in different realms of being and apparently share almost no common traits at all. To put the point in less ontological and more respectable modern terms, there are different language systems when we speak of the church, and they have no discoverable interrelation. In order partly to dispel this confusion, let us begin to sort out the three most pervasive levels or systems of language concerned and then outline the reasons, as one observer sees them, for the unrelatedness that characterizes these levels in contemporary experience.

The first of these three levels one may call "down-to-earth," "concrete," "operational," or possibly "empirical" language. On this level we describe the churches; and we describe them in regard to people, things, and activities that we can see, count, or participate in. Typical questions on this level are: How many people come to church or to Sunday school? How often? How many activities do they participate in once they get there, and of what sort? How much do they contribute? To what extent does the church need to keep up its plant, and how can these numbers, these activities, these contributions—and so this plant—be made to grow? Like any other enterprise in an American city, the church is thought of by many of its laity in the commercial and industrial terms familiar to their experience, and judged by business standards of turnover, budget, and customer satisfaction. Its "products" or "goods" are, as we noted in Chapter IV, the largely cultural values of communal morality, benevolences, and fellowship. Not understanding at all clearly what, if any, the "religious" content of these operations may be, beyond these recognized cultural values, most laymen and indeed most local church boards (the writer has attended two regularly and talked with innumerable ministers about this) leave the mysteries of this peculiar content to the minister and other "religiously inclined types," interpreting the church themselves in these familiar operational and cultural terms. A Southern Baptist clerical friend, to his horror, heard his own role as minister publicly presented by a leading layman as "the local representative of your national organization—you know, like Joe Schmidt over there who represents Hartford Life in Nashville." No wonder expansion and budget count so heavily in the average layman's assessment of the church; or that the mysterious significance of denominational polity is lost on the lay mind!

While it may not seem strange that contemporary laymen see the church in these operational terms of their everyday life, it is surely surprising that many ministers share this statistical language concerning numbers, activities, and plant when they speak of their tasks in the church they serve and their hopes for its future. Even more disheartening, many professional church leaders and most denominational boards reflect the same understanding, and so the same language, though one might have hoped that, for them at least, religious interests would dominate. Their speeches and literature alike are filled almost exclusively with references to the growth, expansion, and stability of the external church. Most ministers, facing interrogation about their work from higher-ups in their denominations, find that a large church role, an expanding budget, or—best of all—the erection of a new plant are considered surer signs of "successful work" than any number of forthright sermons which may have inhibited the growth of the church externally but built up the internal church of faith and love. The church, layman and cleric alike, when it speaks of itself speaks in operational, empirical terms which include little about Word or Sacrament, Bible or salvation, but much about the manifold operations and programs of the institution, the number of people "touched" by these activities, and their friendly, co-operative atmosphere. Small wonder that many laymen know, or at least understand, no other language.

Though he fills an entirely different role from either laymen or professional, there is one other user of the operational language of the first level. This is the sociologist, who, employing his empirical methods, presents us with an exclusively operational and naturalistically causal view of the church. He, too, is concerned with numbers, activities, types and kinds of people, plant, and so forth. But because he wants to understand rather than expand these operations, he tries to discover the "dynamic factors" that cause them rather than the secret "know-how" that will foster them. Investigating the various pressures which its social and economic environments exert on a church, he sees it merely as an institution among others, determined—as are the stock market, the country club, or the political party—by forces in a wider cultural environment. Here our language is at the furthest remove from theological or denominational speech. For to the sociologist's dry, empirical eye our churches, far from being "congregations faithful to their Lord, listening to His Word, illumined by His spirit, and bound together by the ties of selfless love," reveal themselves as groups of bickering as well as co-operating middle-class Americans, pursuing valued but seldom religiously (and certainly not theologically) motivated activities, determined by the same social pressures and suffering under many of the same parochial standards and prejudices as plague their secular communal life. In these descriptions of churches as functioning social institutions, the holy church of biblical-theological discourse never appears at all—nor is it likely that it ever could.

Equally far from the church of empirical description, as a matter of fact, is the church described in our many and varied denominational theories. For under the sharp lens of empirical analysis the differences between our communions tend to dissolve. To most of our laymen and clergy—Catholic, Protestant, or sectarian alike—the church *is* its operations, and these operations are culturally rather than theologically determined and judged; very few distinctions between denominations are seen to be actually there when one looks at the way our local churches operate. Despite differences in theory, most of our communions manifest an identical "denominational" form and much the same mode of operations. Why this should be, the preceding chapters have sought in part to clarify; but I shall have more to say on this point in a moment. Let us merely keep in mind, meanwhile, that one way of talking about the church, shared by laity, active clerics, and secular investigators, is to speak "empirically" of its visible activities, the people who make it up, and the various other social, economic, and physical characteristics it illustrates.

The second level of discourse before us is that of denominational theories of the various communions. Examples are the Baptist theory quoted above, the common Methodist definition of the church as "a community of regenerate Christians going on to perfection," or the Disciples of Christ view that "the Church is guided in faith and practice solely by the precepts of the New Testament." While each of these theories is of great concern to the theologians and apologists of the communion in question, it is virtually inoperative in determining the actual life of local congregations—and little relation is to be found between the definition of congregations as "guided solely by the Bible" or "illumined and directed solely by the Holy Spirit" and the descriptions of churches on the first level of language, noted above. On this second level, the church is viewed in terms of the traditional theology of the group, a theological position which probably reflects its Catholic, Reformation, or sectarian origin, or a combination of these types. These theories view the church in a widely differentiated variety of ways: for example, as a community sanctified by apostolic sacramental graces; as the place where the Word is heard and obeyed; or as a congregation of holy people. While a few laymen and some ministers may be familiar with the phrases and meanings of the traditional theory subscribed to by their church, these theories are, as we have repeatedly seen, unknown to almost all members and to most of the active clergy, and certainly ignored in most church decisions. When one looks at what the church does, as well as what it means to its members, these denominational differences are almost invisible to the naked eye. This was not always so, for these theories did have a definite function in the history of our denominational groups. Now, however, as each unique group has become merely another example of the genus "American denomination," its theological doctrines, like ineffective ghosts from some dim past, float inertly and powerlessly (although appropriately reverenced) over its life. For this reason, except where it had earlier historical importance, this volume has dealt hardly at all with the language of denominational theory about the church.

On a third level appears what we may call "ecumenical language" about the church. Conscious of the remaining disagreements between conflicting denominational theories at the second level, professional churchmen and theologians have recently sought, usually in terms of biblical symbols held in common by all groups, to find a "view of the church" (what in the jargon is called a "church order") that will harmonize all these disparate denominational emphases in one unified doctrinal statement. Thus has appeared that unique series of further abstractions which are associated with ecumenical theology and are so baffling to the earnest inquirer. For here the church is defined and its nature described in terms almost solely of biblical—possibly also historical—symbols, a description designed to express a common "essence" of the church lying behind or within all the lesser and varied denominational definitions. Thus we read that "the church *is* one," that "it is the fellowship of love among all those whose Lord is Christ," that it is a community bound "by its fidelity to his Lordship and its love for one another," that it exists wherever the Word is purely preached and heard and the Sacraments duly administered, and so on. One cannot help wondering what possible entity on land or sea is the referent for these flattering words. Is this the church as it *is,* and if so what does the present tense mean here—for even ecumenical theologians have never found a church in actual practice remotely resembling these descriptions. Does it represent a present Aristotelean "essence" of the church lying within the actual churches; a Platonic idea of the church in heaven in the divine mind; a Kantian law or imperative for the church to realize in future history; or, finally, an eschatological church to come at the end of time? And what sort of existence do these "faithful congregations" enjoy, for surely they are not the people who, with ourselves, make up the church on the corner? What angelic congregations hear the "purely preached Word" and celebrate the "duly enacted Sacraments" that characterize this true church? For little of our preaching and few services can be so defined. Such descriptions of the nature of the church make good theological reading, but one closes the book (especially if one then has to go off to field work among teen-agers) wondering what community in what galaxy has just been described.

What is the difficulty here? What has caused the uniquely abstract and unreal character of this current theological language about the church? First of all, we must insist that there has occurred here what one can only call a "category mistake." That is, symbols expressing the *relation* of God to the life of the existing churches have been mistaken for the substantial *elements* out of which the church is itself composed. Thus in these treatises the church is described, not as if it were composed of finite and sinful men and women living in a particular cultural environment and in some sort of relation to God, but as if the church were made up entirely of biblical symbols—as if "koinonia," "People of God," "lordship of Christ," and so on, were the elements that together made up the church. Now, while in theology it may be appropriate to speak of God solely in the language of biblical and perhaps philosophical symbols, it is extremely dubious whether it is meaningful or accurate to speak of a concrete historical institution made up of visible people exclusively in such symbolic, biblical terms. In the same manner theology has learned, it may be hoped, not to describe "the Christian man" in terms entirely of biblical and theological concepts of grace— for then inevitably a perfect, sinless being is evoked—but rather to describe him as he empirically is, imperfect and sinful, and then relate the concepts of forgiveness and grace to this discovered reality. For unless in both cases empirical description supplements theological categories, the actual human beings who make up the ecclesia, with all their cultural habits, activities, and goals, not to mention their weaknesses and sins, are left completely out of the picture, and quite holy but unactual abstractions result. Clearly biblical and theological symbols have some essential function in Christian thought about the church and about Christians. Equally clearly, however, if we are to avoid comforting but futile abstractions (for, as Kant remarked, "categories without experience are empty"), the function of symbols cannot be that of providing the conceptual materials out of which, as out of bricks, a description of the Christian community is fashioned.

If this category mistake explains the emptiness of these theological views of the church on level three, another sort of mistake explains the aura of irrelevance that accompanies them. As I have noted, one purpose of ecumenical theology has been to bring unity among conflicting denominational theories about the church. From these varied theories one view of the church "common to all" ("order" as opposed to "organization") is developed out of biblical and universally held historical symbols, much as if we dealt with a diversity of denominational species and so were searching for the one underlying ecclesiastical genus. The difficulty, of course, is that in this case the definitions of the species in question no longer apply to or describe the actual particulars. Rather, as we have seen, these denominational theories are themselves already lifeless abstractions separated by historical, social, and cultural changes from the ongoing life of their congregations—and floating above that life largely unknown, ignored, or inapplicable. This ecumenical "common denominator" is simply an abstraction from previous abstractions, a universal derived from preceding universals which themselves no longer apply to anything. As in a kind of modern Pseudo-Dionysian hierarchy of being,[1] these ghostly concepts of "true clerical orders," "faithful congregations," "preached Word," and "en-

[1] Pseudo-Dionysius the Areopagite was, apparently, a Syrian monk or ecclesiastic of the late fifth century A.D. who wrote mystical and philosophical treatises which had great significance for Greek and medieval Western theology. Under the clear influence of Plotinus and his follower Proclus (c. 430 A.D.), Dionysius saw reality as a ladder of spiritual and divine realms descending from the unnamable, superessential Godhead down to earth, and salvation as the ascent of the soul through these levels or hierarchies of sacred beings back up to the One again. Our reference in the text is to thoughts contained in his treatises, "The Ecclesiastical Hierarchies" and "The Celestial Hierarchies" (*De ecclestiastica hierarchia* and *De coelesti hierarchia*), in which the earthly ecclesiastical hierarchies of deacons, priests, and bishops with their sacraments and rites are duplicated in the spiritual realm above them by three triads of divine hierarchical beings: Principalities, Archangels, and Angels; Dominions, Powers and Authorities; and highest of all, Cherubim, Seraphim, and Thrones. The same stages of purification, illumination, and perfection through which the earthly believer must pass to begin his ascent on high are also carried over into these upper divine realms, where in spiritual form rites cor-

acted sacraments" hover over the already tenuous denominational concepts, which in turn hover unnoticed over the remarkably similar operations of actual churches. These are some of the reasons why this level of discourse has also not appeared in this book, and why nowhere in these pages is there a strictly theological definition of the nature of the church. The air is too thin way up there even for this theologian's speculation—though many ecumenical committees have toiled endless hours on these issues of what I can only describe as "rarified order."

The consequences of this three-way split of language systems concerning the church are of course manifold and serious. They result in types of literature and discussion about church problems which are quite unrelated to one another and seem, in their present disjointed state, almost without effect on the life of the churches. On the one hand there are the purely secular sociological inquiries. These are, of course, immensely informative and invaluable concerning the practice and habits, the dynamic factors and social pressures, that characterize the contemporary church. Since, however, they perforce employ only the most strictly empirical methods, and since most such inquirers are more interested in the social dynamics of the institution than in its religious structure and character, these investigations tend to pass right over the religious core of the church and, except by implication, tell us little of what goes on in it religiously. We are informed what sort of social institution it is, how it functions socially, and what its measurable social effects are; but what sort of *church* it is—that we do not learn. On the other hand, treatises in terms of theological theory—either denominational or biblical and ecumenical—seem merely to shuffle the traditional symbols around, rearranging them in new combinations or giving them ever new connotations. Since no one knows (or even asks) what entities, besides the symbols themselves, these discussions are *about*, they too fail to tell us much either theologically or sociologically about the church as it exists on earth.

What is needed, clearly, is twofold. First of all there is re-

---

responding to earthly sacraments and other liturgical acts are performed. Above the visible, earthly church, therefore, ascends a ghostly ladder where are reduplicated in *geistliche* perfection what is done materially here below.

quired an empirical investigation that seeks to uncover what the actual religious reality of the contemporary denominational church is. What sort of religion—if there be any—is there in our churches, in terms of belief, experience, worship, and behavior? What sort of *churches* are they? Such knowledge can come only through empirical inquiry (using that word in the widest sense of a study of what is actually found by investigation to be the case). To uncover the religious core of the life of our churches, such an inquiry must also be theologically informed and motivated, and thus capable of defining and locating its religious object. In such an investigation theological doctrines, both denominational and biblical, about what the church is should be used to inform the questions asked rather than to provide content for answers received. Only in that way can the churches' actual, instead of their ideal, religious character become visible to us. In this inquiry such questions as the following might be posed: How does the Bible function, if at all, in the minds of church people; do they read, do they know, do they understand it? How do their beliefs function, if at all; are Christian concepts known, understood, believed? How do standards of "Christian behavior" function? What do they think they ought to do? What do they think they ought to *think* they ought to do? And are the things condemned in these standards regarded as *really* wrong; and do they *really* admire the virtues there praised? How does worship function, if at all? What does it mean, if anything? What good is it? What good do people get out of it; what good do they think they *ought* to get out of it? What do the sacraments mean? What do they do, if anything? What is their value? What, finally, is the church *for*? What is its value? How does it save you, if it does— and so on. Several studies have begun such investigations (e.g., the Obenhaus study of Corn County), but at present, while everyone has personal guesses about the answers to such questions, and many of us have read the results of innumerable student surveys of their churches on these matters, there are no data with wide enough range to permit *knowledge* of the whole situation of the church in America.

Secondly, what is needed is that these data be given both an historical and a theological analysis. Both perspectives are important if we are to understand the American church as a church.

The roots of its present religious situation lie in the confluence of its own past with its present environment, and only by careful historical and cultural analysis can one unearth the factors that have brought it, in its present structure, into being. (One thinks especially here of the work of Sydney Mead.) Also this religious structure must be subjected to theological analysis—that is, understood in relation to the great symbols, both biblical and historical, that give theological structure to the church. While these symbols do not compose the church as if it were made up of them rather than of people, they do have some essential relation to the church, and thus the church cannot be understood or thought of without them. What is that relation?

The theory about theological language and the church that has informed these chapters is that biblical and theological symbols (the People of God, the New Israel, the lordship of Christ, the Word of God, the Body of Christ, and so on) point or refer to the dimension of transcendence or of the holy in the church's life —to the ways in which God works within the church in judgment and in grace. And the belief about the nature of the church, its ontology, so to speak, that underlies this interpretation of theological language is that the church is a human and therefore social community among other social communities, but one with a peculiar vertical or religious relation within which God works quite uniquely for the salvation of the total human community —in preaching, mission, worship, sacraments, and the behavior patterns of its life. The biblical symbols are related to this social community as expressions of this transcendent dimension; as witnesses, on the basis of the divine promise, to the possibility of the holy within the community's life, and as indicating the means through which the divine action takes place, or can take place, within the community. If this is so, then the "docetic" error of describing the church on the basis of biblical symbols alone becomes clear: for what expresses the transcendent or vertical dimension of a social community is then taken as a complete description of the elements that make up the community. There has been, however, no biblical revelation of what the people of the churches or their cultural habits are to be like; there has been only a revelation of what God asks of such a community and of how He promises to work within it. Thus if we would find out what the church as a human and religious community is, we must look at its actual life and behavior, and not deduce them from ways in which our Lord has promised to be in our midst.

In a halting and surely preliminary way, this book has sought to begin the type of empirical, historical, and theological analysis envisioned here. On the basis of his own experience, of innumerable studies of local churches by his students, and of such formal studies as are available, the writer has attempted a study of the *actual* religious structure of the modern denomination, not only as a form of the church, but as a community of behavior, beliefs, and worship. Next, some of the historical and social factors that brought about this religious situation have been outlined and their influence on the religious life within the churches discussed. Finally, this actual religious structure—what I have called the denomination—was more closely scrutinized in relation to three central biblical symbols, each pointing to a promised means of divine activity in and on the community. And the question was asked: In what ways can this community, as it now lives and functions, be made more open to the work of God in its midst, in behavior, belief, and worship? The conviction that lies back of this analysis is that the denomination as we know it represents a new form of the church, both sociologically and religiously, and that this new form contains great potentialities as well as great dangers. Further, this form has only been obscured by denominational theories which describe the actual churches in totally ideal, inaccurate, and so irrelevant terms. What is imperative, therefore, if the dangers inherent in the denominational form are to be avoided, is that this new religious structure be carefully looked at, honestly studied, and above all, candidly admitted by churchmen. Only then will the actual contemporary church be clearly enough understood so that needed changes in its organization and its habits can be made. While men cannot by their works save the church, by their blind devotion to older forms and their dogged insistence upon irrelevancies, they seem able to reduce the saving work of God through the churches from a flood to a trickle. To discourage this blind devotion and concentrate attention upon our real problems, I have sought to give this empirical, historical, and theological analysis of the actual social community we label the church. It is hoped that far fuller and broader empirical stud-

ies of the contemporary denomination will enlarge the work of
Obenhaus and Winter, and that far better historical and theological analyses will replace this brief one.

In this essay I have made a good deal of the wide gulf between
denominational theories about the church and the layman's and
the sociologist's language about it. All through this text I have
sought to show that a careful empirical analysis of the religious
structure of the churches of any denomination (i.e., of their systems of authority, patterns of belief and behavior, habits of worship, and goals and values) bears almost no relation to the
descriptions of the church which the several denominational theories foster, when they think about their church and its problems.
The result has been that theological language about the church,
whether denominational or ecumenical, has seemed to refer to
some other church than the actual one, and to be therefore
irrelevant and impotent, providing no standards for actual preaching and behavior, no inward meanings for worship and sacraments, and no relevant goals for the churches' activities and life.

Since this wide gap between theory and practice is such a
significant feature of our situation, it will bear fuller concluding
discussion. The disjunction between theological language about
the church and language descriptive of its nature in practice was,
it seems, by no means always so evident or so wide as at present. There was in fact a time when the theological definitions of
the church which we have called "denominational theories"
played a much more active and therefore much less abstract and
confused role. Each denomination in church history at first appeared because of some new view of the church and its gospel
which that group sought to embody as an actual, visible, historic expression or example of what it viewed as the "true
church." Thus originally the "theologies of the church" on the
denominational level were *prescriptive* statements directed
toward the actual churches, programs for their reformation.
They were, in other words, not abstract definitions but practical,
albeit theological, statements which intended to outline, and thus
effect, concrete changes in the life of an actual congregation or
body of congregations, and so to refashion the preaching, liturgy,
and behavior of that historical group along certain definitely

specified lines. They were not so much definitions of an abstract theological entity named "church," as rules of action for actual churches. For example, at the Reformation the defining ecclesiological phrase "where the Word is preached" functioned in a quite concrete and not at all abstract manner. Connoting as it did a very definite theological system (i.e., that of Calvinism or Lutheranism) it implied in great detail a certain definite theological content in the actual preaching to specific congregations, and thus provided the terms in which heresy could be clearly defined and eliminated. Correspondingly, the theological symbol of the church as a "regenerate community" connoted a certain specific code of moral behavior, definite enough to discriminate among members, with the ultimate goal (wherever necessary) of expulsion. Thus the definition of the church as "where the Word is preached" *meant* "that and no other is a church whose preaching embodies Calvin's theology and no other theology— and every church must be guided accordingly." And the definition "the church is a regenerate community" *meant* "the church is a community whose members abide by such and such a definite code of behavior and no other—and so every church must obey this standard." In each case the intent or purpose of the theory was the active reformation of the historical group's life along the lines here theologically described. In the past, therefore, denominational language has been both specific in content and prescriptive in intention. It expressed the clear goal of becoming, once the intended reforms implied were enacted, *descriptive* of the life of the actual congregation—of becoming, that is to say, identical with language at level one, language that any observer of the visible church might use about it. Whether or not any visible church could ever so embody its ideals that theological language could be called actually descriptive is dubious. Nevertheless, the intention to be such is clear enough, and the concreteness of the language made this logically possible.

This denominational language today has in almost every case neither such concrete implications nor such definite, practical intention. The ecclesiastical theories of most communions determine the theological content of very few of their sermons and the characteristic behavior of even fewer of their laymen. Nor, even more significantly, do they remotely intend to do so. For lying behind the symbolic phrases of most communions there is no longer any one definite system of theology, nor any one specific code of behavior, and even if there were, it is doubtful whether anyone would be particularly interested in applying them as concrete standards. Certainly few present denominational groups intend to embark upon frequent heresy trials or to publish regular excommunication edicts when they speak of their churches as places where "the Word is heard" or as communities "of regenerate people." Thus current denominational language intends to prescribe for no actual congregation's life; in intent it is no longer descriptive of any actual community. On the contrary, this language has become what we have called "abstract." This does not mean that it is abstract because it is theological, for theological language about the church has its own valid role in describing actual communities in their relation to God. It is abstract because its intended referent is purely conceptual. That is to say, instead of referring to an actual community, its words point only to "our denominational view of the church," a nonempirical and so presumably nonexistent theological entity or idea. Most denominational theorizing is about this idea (not about the churches), and as I have noted, ecumenical theology tends to abstract even further from these denominational ideas into the one supreme and unified idea of the church. Thus occurs the fatal split in language systems mentioned earlier: between denominational and ecumenical languages which describe only abstract conceptual entities or "views of the church," on the one hand, and the operational language that describes our actual congregations, on the other.

When one asks why this disjunction has in the recent history of these groups so vastly widened, the answers are, as this book has sought to show, largely historical and sociocultural in character. Let me summarize these two points briefly. First of all, most of the groups which at present share what I have called the denominational form of church life, with its partly church-type and partly sect-type characteristics, originally embodied vastly different forms of the church. Many of them, and on these we have concentrated, were sectarian in their original form. Others such as the Roman Catholic, the Anglican, and the Lutheran, had originally the church-type form. In joining American society, and in the consequent modification of their forms, they gradually ceased to embody the structures contained in their own inherited views of themselves. Thus, while the definition of the Baptist churches as "covenanted, autonomous congregations of regenerate Christians" might have been prescriptive language a century or more ago, determining not only the actual polity but also the actual behavior and social character of these congregations, such a definition seems anachronistic and irrelevant now that these groups have taken on a form with the formerly church-type characteristics of a secularized laity, a large centralized organization, and the goals of expansion and stability. Correspondingly, older church-type churches such as the Orthodox, the Roman, and the Episcopal have likewise changed as they became denominations, and they too have taken on a surprising number of sectarian or denominational traits. Since, however, most of them still retain some separated elements of the holy—priestly and sacramental, if not dogmatic—they have not yet completely adopted the full denominational form of their fellow communions, and for this reason retain their own peculiar strengths and weaknesses in the American scene.

Now the point is that despite these historical changes the denominational theologies of the churches have not changed. They still describe the church in their older sectarian, Reformation, or Catholic modes as if nothing had happened sociologically at all. Yet none of the religious elements, none of those areas of church life where grace is received or experienced, have remained the same; in belief, in behavior, in preaching and worship our denominations have ceased to fit their own self-descriptions. Hence the dichotomy between an older theory that once applied to a now vanished community, and a present actuality that has been substantially transformed. To put this into current ecumenical jargon, at the beginning of their life the "organization" of these groups was formed at least in part by their theological conceptions of church "order." Now their organizational patterns have undergone a radical sociological change, while the "order" has remained the same, becoming, like most things historical, a concern mainly for denominational historians and theologians but unknown to the majority of active clergy and lay folk.

There has also been a complementary process at work in the

culture as a whole that has encouraged this separation between descriptive, empirical operational language and theological language. I refer once more to the secularization of life generally, and so of the church and of churchmen in particular. It is even harder to read the minds and hearts of laymen of the past than of the present concerning their religion, since only leaders of one sort or another have ordinarily written down their inward thoughts and beliefs, and we have been left no empirical surveys of the religion of past congregations to guide us. From the documents of the past, however, one cannot help feeling that, while the churches and their coffers may have been no fuller then, at least there was more knowledge of and concern for what we have called the transcendent dimensions of the church than is true now. Whatever the various sins and weaknesses of past churchmen, the facts indicate that the average man in the pew cared more than does his modern counterpart about what sort of doctrine he heard from the pulpit, and about what the sacraments meant and accomplished, what church law required of his own and his fellows' behavior, what sort of "experiences of religion" might be afforded him, and certainly his own final status before the throne of the Almighty. Thus, while many undoubtedly had a merely conventional interest in the church, many also had, pretended to have, or thought they ought to have, a "religious interest." For them, not only was the theological language by which their denomination understood and described itself intelligible—most of them could state *why* they were Presbyterian, Lutheran, or Baptist, and many were willing to suffer for it—but they also believed that this language should be concretely determinative of their church's life. It was in their minds prescriptive language, intending to be descriptive. Since they understood themselves and their church *religiously*, they did not view theological language about the church as either unintelligible or irrelevant, but rather as the obvious and natural way in which to talk about the church as a religious institution.

Everything that our "empirical" analysis of present church life has indicated, however, shows that this religious dimension has in large part dropped out of our denominational life, for much of the laity and the clergy alike. Issues of belief, of doctrine, or of behavior are no longer central or even real for our church life;

and few seem to know or experience any religious elements in worship or in sacrament, or in personal life within the community of the church. As investigation after investigation shows beyond dispute, all elements of former church life that could be called "religious," all media of the vertical dimension of the community's existence—yes, even all that could be called a vehicle of explicit relation to God, have apparently receded in significance within the life of the church. If religion as a word, and theological language as a mode of speech, point to the vertical, Godward dimension of the church's existence, then it is the disappearance of that religious dimension in our century that has in large part caused the irrelevance and unintelligibility of theological language about the church. For if the church's life has in fact (and this seems to be the case) become dominated by secular activities with secular goals, then it is quite understandable that secular operational language about the church should be used by laity, clergy, and scientific observer alike, and that any other form of language should become unintelligible for both the ordinary layman and the active minister.

That this loss of the religious dimension of the church's life has not in fact caused a decline in the popularity of the church is as surprising as it is undeniable. I have sought to explain this by showing that secular social values which were always present in the life of the church have now come to the fore and replaced religious values as the primary bonds of loyalty and support. Like all else in our age—politics, economics, education, and the like —the church has been secularized and yet has continued to function, but now in a secularized form. The difference with these other social communities is that, while they have long since dispensed with their earlier religious or theological foundations, the denominations have not, but have kept them there as the guiding channels for self-understanding. The split in language systems I have described in this chapter is the reflection in the area of discourse of this general drift of the life of the church away from its theological and religious foundations. The meaninglessness of theological language about the church represents in our word usage that same disappearance of the holy that I have analyzed and traced in preceding chapters as the main clue to modern religion. For the purpose of theological discourse is to point to, express, and so far as is possible make intelligible the appearance of the holy in our experience. If the holy seems not at all to appear, then it is natural that discourse about it should seem irrelevant, meaningless, and empty.

If this is so, then clearly this crisis in discourse is more than a purely theological or linguistic problem, and its answer must be found on deeper levels than are reached by merely theological or semantic solutions. The holy must relate itself again to our total existence, both personal and communal, if any reunion of the operational and theological language of the church is to take place. As I noted in the first chapter, some commentators have found an answer to this crisis of separation by seeking to divest the church and its teachings of the transcendent dimension, since the latter no longer seems intelligible to our secular age. If God is dead in and to the minds of twentieth-century people, then (they say in effect) He is dead in truth. And because of this death the church had best relinquish its Godward dimension and its Godward language. Very much as the present book seeks now to advise the churches, after sociological change, to reassess and even transform their older denominational descriptions of themselves, so now because of the change from a religious to a secular culture, these thinkers advise us to abandon the religious aspects of church and theology alike.

Of the secularism of our age and its influence on church life and language there can be little doubt. This book has sought above all to document that fact. But the seeming irrelevance of God to our time and the corresponding feelings of emptiness concerning Him are no proof either that He is in fact dead or that we do not need Him, despite our good opinions of ourselves. The salvation of a church that has almost lost its Lord lies not in forgetting Him, but in finding Him again in its life. If that is to be possible, however, we must be free to experiment, not only with our theological language and our forms of mission and service, but even more with the structures of church life and organization which we have inherited from an age whose customs and spiritual forms were vastly different from our own.

Index

ABRAHAM, 6 f.
ADAM, K., 6 n.
AMALGAMATION WITH WORLD, 15 f.; conservative form, 35 ff., 44 ff.; and Enlightenment, 29 f.; and evangelicalism, 33 f.; and fellowship, 68 ff.; liberal form, 47 f., 49 f.; and Word, 80
AMERICAN CHURCH: conservative form, 35 ff.; its dangers, 54 f.; its denominational form, 4, 56 f.; and Enlightenment, 29 f.; and evangelicalism, 32 f.; and koinonia, 66 f., 68 f.; liberal form, 47 f.; its problems, 57 f., 116; and secularism, 99; and social changes, 36 ff., 43 f., 57 f., 67 f., 89 f., 110 ff., 116
AMISH, 7, 18
ANABAPTISTS, 7, 8 n., 11 n., 67, 83 n., 110 n.
ANDERSON, B. W., 61 n.
ANGLICANISM, see Episcopalianism
APOSTOLICITY, 5; its Protestant form, 77
ARCHITECTURE, CHURCH, 109
AUGUSTINE, 2 n., 38 n., 42 n., 65 n.
AUTHORITY IN THE CHURCH, 7 n., 57 f.; of clergy, 84 f.; in the denomination, 84; and the Enlightenment, 31; in ethics, 45 f.; and the truth, 96; and the Word, 75, 91 ff.

BAPTISM, 51; as fellowship with Christ, 106; as material symbol, 120; in sects, 8 n.
BAPTISTS, 7, 14 n., 18, 51, 68, 91, 143
BERGMAN, I., 22 n.
BIBLE, 3, 58; as authority, 97 f.; in conservative Protestantism, 44; in denomination, 85 ff.; and the lay mind, 89 ff., 96 f., 111 f.; in sects, 7 n., 10 f., 85; and theology, 96 f.
BIBLICAL SYMBOLS, 4, 58 f.; Body of Christ, 59, 104 ff.; Christ as Lord, 59, 75 ff.; and ecumenical language, 134; and empirical language, 134; their function, 58 f., 138 f.; and the Holy, 58 f., 138 f.; and Jesus Christ, 106 n.; People of God, 59 ff.; role in the church, 92 n.
BODY OF CHRIST, 2 n., 5 n., 42 n., 59, 104 ff.; as broken, 125
BONHOEFFER, D., 23 n., 53 n.
BOONE, P., 16 n.
BROWN, R. M., 66 n.
BUICKS, clerical, 17 n.
BULTMANN, R., 23 n., 53 n.
BURNABY, J., 42 n., 65 n.

CALVIN, J., 6 n., 11 n., 60 n., 76 n., 78 n., 119 n., 120 n., 121, 125 n.
CALVINISM, 6, 11 n., 30 n., 31 n., 109 n.
CAMPBELL, A. and T., 7 n.
CASSIRER, E., 29 n., 31 n.
CATHOLICISM, 4, 5 n., 11 n., 40, 59, 67, 109 n., 142; and conservative Protestantism, 36 f., 43 f.; as prophetic critic, 46, 84
CHADWICK, H., 94 n.
CHRIST, see Jesus Christ
CHRISTIAN ETHIC: in Catholicism, 4 f.; in conservative Protestantism, 36 ff., 44 f.; in denominations, 17 f., 70 ff., 101 f.; double standard, 36 f.; and Enlightenment, 29 f.; in evangelicalism, 32 f.; in liberalism, 48 f., 51 f.; in sects, 10 ff.; two-realms, 38 f.
CHURCH: American form, 4, 15 f., 26, 28; amalgamation with world, 4, 14 f., 88 f.; and Biblical symbols, 58 f., 138 f.; as Body of Christ, 2 n., 104 ff.; as broken body, 125; as church-type, 4 ff.; and communism, 54 f.; as a community, 59 f., 102 f.; conservative form, 33 ff.; and denominational theories, 132 f., 135 f.; as denomination, 15 f., 57; and ecumenical language, 133 f., 135 f.; and empirical inquiry, 136 f.; and fellowship, 67 ff., 89; and its gnosis, 94 f.; and God's will, 2, 60, 81 f., 138 f.; and the Holy, 3, 5 f., 9 f., 12 ff., 15, 44 f., 52 f., 57 f., 71 f., 75 f., 107 ff., 125 f., 138 f.; and Jesus Christ, 59, 62 f., 65 f., 75 f.; liberal form, 47 ff.; as local congregation, 25 ff.; and its mission, 63 n.f.; and its moral law, 64 f., 70 f.; as the People of God, 59 f., 66 f.; its current popularity, 87 f.; its problems, 57 f.; as prophetic critic, 45 f.; and secularism, 22 f., 143 f.; as sect-type, 7 ff.; separation from world, 5 ff., 8 f., 10 ff., 15 ff., 29 f., 32 f., 52 f., 56 f.; and social gospel, 71 f.; tension with world, 1 f., 5, 8, 23 f., 28; and theological language, 128 ff.; and the truth, 85 ff., 89 f., 97 f.; and the Word, 75 f.; and worship, 108 ff.
CHURCH-TYPE, 4 ff.; in conservative Protestantism, 35 ff.; in the denomination, 15 f., 35 ff.; in liberalism, 50 f.
CHURCHES OF CHRIST, 7, 16 n., 18, 47
CLEMENT OF ALEXANDRIA, 94 n.
CLERGY: their authority, 84 ff.; in conservative Protestantism, 36 f.; in the

Biblical References